TECHNIQUES

Every drawing or painting depends on a number of choices. Some of the most important decisions are made before anything is put down on paper or canvas. Viewpoint, color, balance, perspective, and tone are factors that dictate the composition, providing the foundation of a successful work. "Putting it all together" is a process that begins with the eye and moves on through the sketchbook. With this foundation in place you can begin to practice the drawing and painting techniques to achieve the effects you have chosen. And even if you take a wrong turn, there is usually a chance to make things right, or at least to take your work in a new direction.

GETTING STARTED

It is no wonder that the early Renaissance painters acclaimed the newly developed oil paint as "a most beautiful invention." After the rigors of the demanding and difficult egg tempera medium, it must have seemed like manna from heaven – so much easier to use, so versatile, so colorful. By our standards, of course, it was not very easy to use in those days – there were no handy tubes or painting boards, pigments had to be laboriously ground by hand and canvases or panels made and primed before the painting could start. The first oil paints were similar in handling to their tempera predecessors, but gradually artists began to understand the nature of the new invention and exploit it to the fullest to produce works of originality and excitement. They are still doing so today – oil paint has never lost its popularity, and modern paint manufacturers are constantly developing new and better colors, mediums, and painting surfaces so that we can express ourselves freely, secure in the confidence that our paintings will not discolor or crack with age.

One of the main advantages of oil paints from the novice's point of view is that they dry slowly and can be used opaquely. There isn't much you can do with an unsuccessful watercolor except throw it away and start again, but the obligingly thick consistency of oils allows you to overpaint mistakes as often as you like, changing and improving your drawing,

SELF PORTRAIT by Paul Cézanne, c.1872

Cézanne used his paint thickly in most but not all areas of the face. Much of it has been applied wet into wet, allowing the colors to blend into one another on the canvas.

colors, and forms until you begin to see your painting take shape in the way you envisioned. Because it dries slowly, you can manipulate the paint on the canvas, moving it around to create new and interesting effects. In fact, you can use it in an almost endless variety of ways, putting it on thick with a knife; in small, delicate brush strokes; in thin, transparent layers, or even painting with a rag or blending colors together with your fingers.

LEARNING FROM THE MASTERS

This section of the book outlines some of the best-known and most useful techniques in oil painting. But bear in mind that the two best ways of learning to use paints are first, doing it yourself and second, studying the methods of other artists first hand. All the great painters of the past learned from their predecessors – several of the Impressionists used to copy the work of the Old Masters. So if you have a chance to visit art galleries, take a hard, analytical look at the work of any artists you particularly admire. Most oil paintings only achieve their full effect when viewed from a distance, but if you then go up close you will see all sorts of fascinating technical details. You may notice that a

DR. GACHET by Vincent van Gogh, 1890

Van Gogh worked very fast, painting directly onto the canvas, with no underpainting. Although the paint is thick throughout the picture, there is little overpainting – notice how you can see the bare canvas between the brush strokes on the sleeve.

color that appeared flat is actually broken up into separate brush strokes, or that the paint is very thin in some areas and thick in others, with highlights put on with a painting knife. Although it is important to evolve your own individual methods and ways of looking at things, it is a pity to let the experiments and experiences of earlier artists go to waste.

BLENDING

Blending is the process of merging one color or tone into another so that no sharp boundary is formed. It is used when soft effects are needed; for example, the gradation of a rich blue sky from deep color to pale; clouds; subtle light and shade effects in a portrait and so on.

One of the best "implements" to use for such effects is the fingers. Whether to blend colors or not and the degree to which you should take the blending depends on the way you use brushwork and on the particular passage being dealt with. An artist who favors highly finished, detailed work may create imperceptibly smooth gradations across large areas of his canvas. At the other extreme, one who paints in loose brush strokes may restrict blending to the placing of one color up to and beyond the boundary with the next one.

In most cases the colors to be blended will be closely related, as they will represent contiguous areas of a single form, and will mix to give a true blend of intermediate colors. Colors that mix to create a completely new color cannot be blended satisfactorily; for example, blue cannot be blended with yellow since a band of green appears where the two colors overlap.

1 Here the artist uses a No. 4 flat bristle brush to apply two broad bands of color (cadmium red and cadmium yellow) adjacent to each other.

2 Using a soft, long-haired brush, the artist "knits" the two colors together where they meet, using short, smooth strokes. For best results, always work the lighter color into the darker one.

3 The finished effect. The colors are blended together softly, but the liveliness of the brush marks prevents the area from looking too "perfect" and monotonous.

In the painting below the blending technique has been used to achieve soft gradations of color and tone. Some darker patches of paint have been "pulled" further down into the foreground to give the impression of ripples. These echo the deliberately rough blending in the sky, which helps to unify the whole. In this case the boundary between sea and sky has been left unblended, but on a hazy day this area might also need blending.

31

BROKEN COLOR

HAYMAKER'S FIELD by Christopher Baker

Patches of bright scarcely mixed paint are built up into a mosaic of color. At a distance the colors merge together to create a scintillating, light-filled image.

Broken color, put at its simplest, means color that is not applied flat and is not blended. In most oil paintings, at any rate those in which brushwork forms a feature, the color is to some extent broken, but it can be done in a more planned and deliberate way.

OPTICAL MIXING

The English landscape painter John Constable (1776–1837) was one of the first to realize that colors, particularly greens, appeared more vivid if they were applied as small strokes of varied hues placed side by side. The Impressionists took the idea further, often juxtaposing small dabs of blue, green, and violet in shadow areas. When viewed from the correct distance they fused together to read as one color while retaining a lively, flickering brilliance that could not be achieved by flat color. Like Constable, they worked directly from nature, and the method, because it cut down on pre-mixing time, allowed them to complete paintings very rapidly before the light changed.

George Seurat (1859–1891), who was influenced by scientific discoveries about light and color, further refined the theory of optical mixing in his technique of pointillism.

MODIFICATIONS

The essence of optical mixing is to keep all the colors relatively bright and pure and the brush strokes as small as possible, but this is not the only way to "break" color. A painting consisting mainly of muted hues, such as a townscape or winter landscape, can be enlivened by an adaptation of the same approach. This is best done with a square-ended brush and involves placing larger brush strokes of several separate but related hues side by side with no blending, giving a mosaic-like effect. This is a good method for flat surfaces such as walls that might otherwise run the risk of drabness, and the square brush strokes can also give a textured impression.

WORKING METHODS

Both broken-color methods take some practice, as very careful mixing and assessment of color are needed. In optical mixing, for instance, the introduction of a pale yellow or a bright red into a mid-toned blue/green/brown color area would immediately destroy the effect, as the difference in tone would be too great.

The same applies to the related method – the colors must be close in tone and chosen so that they have a definite relationship to one another. It can he helpful to work on a colored ground, because any small areas left uncovered between brush strokes will help to unify the pictures – patches of white have exactly the opposite effect unless all the applied colors are very pale.

The paint must be fairly thick so it does not run and allows the brush strokes to retain their shape. Brushes must be carefully washed between each stroke or group of strokes, or the new color will be sullied by traces of the earlier one left on the brush.

Broken color effects can also be created by dry brush, glazing, and scumbling, all of which are ways of working wet on dry to modify existing colors.

ON HIGH GROUND
by Juliette Palmer

There is some blurring of paint wet into wet here, but on the whole each brush mark retains its own identity. The patches of color are relatively large, so optical color mixing does not occur, but the effect is livelier than flat color.

ALLA PRIMA

Alla prima is an Italian term meaning "at first," and it describes paintings completed in one session. This necessarily involves working wet into wet rather than allowing a first layer to dry before others are added. The essential characteristic of *alla prima* is that there is no initial underpainting as such, although artists often make a rapid underdrawing in pencil or charcoal to establish the main lines.

After the introduction of tubed paint in the mid-19th century, artists were able to work outdoors more easily. This *plein air* painting, as it is called, first undertaken by painters such as Constable (1776–1837), Corot (1796–1875), and later the Impressionists, established the rapid and direct *alla prima* approach as an acceptable technique. Hitherto oil painting had been largely a studio activity as pigment had to be ground by hand, and paintings were built up slowly in a series of layers.

The direct method creates a lively and free effect that is seldom seen in more deliberate studio paintings. This is certainly true of Constable, whose small landscape sketches done on the spot have much more immediacy and vigor than his larger works such as *The Haywain*.

Working *alla prima* requires some confidence, as each patch of color is laid down more or less as it will appear in the finished picture. Any modifications and reworking must be kept to a minimum so that the fresh effect is not destroyed.

It is a good idea to use a limited palette, as too wide a choice of colors may tempt you to put in too much detail – there is no room for nonessentials in *alla prima* painting. It is usually easiest to leave the lightest and darkest passages to the end so that the brush strokes used for these lie undisturbed on top of adjacent colors without mixing and muddying.

1 Because it is difficult to get ellipses right, these were first drawn with pencil. The next stage was to block in some of the shaded areas with cobalt blue and the tablecloth with ocher, which helped to establish the feel of the composition. This photo shows some of the basic colors being laid in with rather thicker paint.

2 The tablecloth has been loosely painted and the darker tones of the fruit developed. The red stripe around the bowl is crucial to the composition, so it is painted next, in a mixture of cadmium red and alizarin crimson. On the fruit, intermediate colors have been introduced between the darks and the lights without blending their boundaries. The final highlight has now been scumbled onto the orange, using a round bristle brush. The other pieces of fruit are treated in a similar way, taking care that the intermediate colors successfully link the dark with the light areas.

3 The tablecloth has been completed, and the shadows of the bowl, peppermill, and pear added. A final sable is used for laying small highlights on the peppermill in thick, undiluted paint.

4 After approximately two hours' work, the painting is complete. Although certain areas have been modified by painting wet into wet, the majority of the paintwork remains exactly as it was first applied.

COLORED GROUNDS

Many artists like to paint on a pure white surface, as the light reflected back through the paint gives a quality of luminosity to the work. The Impressionists favored white grounds for this reason, but they can be inhibiting, particularly for beginners. It is difficult to assess colors against white, and there is a tendency to paint in too light a key, as almost any color looks too dark by contrast. Another drawback is that when working outdoors the white surface can be dazzling, which can cause an over-hasty rush to obliterate all white areas.

A colored ground will be closer to the average tone of the final picture, making it easier to judge both colors and lights and darks from the outset. Mid-tones are the easiest to work on as you can paint toward light or dark with equal ease. If you paint over a very dark ground (called a bole) it follows that you will continually be adding lighter tones, culminating in highlights of thick, opaque paint.

1 The artist has chosen a mid-tone ocher ground as a basis for working toward both light and dark. He has begun the painting with the deep shadow areas.

2 One advantage of a colored ground is that the painting never looks too "unfinished," even in the early stages. This is especially helpful to the beginner as it avoids the discouragement of large areas of unpainted white canvas.

3 Patches of lighter paint have now been introduced. The artist will leave unpainted those areas approximating to the ground in tone and color. At this stage it is possible to decide which they are to be.

Coloring a ground, whether canvas or board, is easily done by laying a thin layer of paint, diluted with white spirit, over the white priming. Acrylic can also be used, in this case diluted with water. The ground can be any color, but the most-used are subdued hues – browns, ochers, blue-grays, greens, or even reds. The choice of color is important as it acts as a background for applied colors to play against and thus effects the color-key of the finished picture. Some artists like a ground that contrasts or is complementary to the dominant color, for instance, a warm red-brown shows up green foliage while an ocher could enhance the brilliance of blue in a seascape. Others prefer a matching ground—blue-gray for a seascape, or brown for a figure painting. Rubens (1577–1640) always painted his figure compositions on a yellow-brown ground, leaving areas unpainted to stand as the mid-tones. Allowing the ground color to show through in this way is still common practice, whether the color is contrasting or harmonizing. This helps to unify the picture, as small areas of the same color recur throughout.

4 This detail shows how the loose brush-work follows the directions of the forms. Some areas of the ground are still to be painted over, but those on the fallen tree, representing flakes of bark, will be left as they are.

5 Small areas of the ground remain exposed throughout the picture, their golden color helping to unify the composition and contrasting with the cool greens and grays. These might otherwise have become over-dominant.

UNDERPAINTING

Not all artists begin their work with an underpainting, as this depends very much on individual ways of working. In the *alla prima* method, for example, there is usually no underpainting, and perhaps only a very sketchy underdrawing to serve as a guide for areas of color. In the more deliberate and considered type of painting, however, underpainting can play an important part, as the idea is to leave parts of it visible in the final painting. In this respect it serves the same function as a colored ground, but whereas the latter helps to unify the whole picture, an underpainting establishes the main dark and light areas, and the colors of these are chosen to act as a foil to the final layers.

Usually only a few fairly neutral colors are used, thinly diluted with turpentine or white spirit. Little or no oil should be added at this stage; the thicker and oilier layers are built up later.

1 Fast-drying cobalt blue diluted with a large quantity of white spirit was used for this preliminary underpainting. In this case it was not intended to play an important part in the finished painting; its main aim was to act as a guide by segregating the dark and light passages within the intricate pattern of leaves, stalks, and reflections.

2 The dark background at left is blocked in with thin, lean paint. This is essentially a continuation of the underpainting, and it will still be visible through several glazed layers in the finished picture. Further broad blocking in is done with rather less diluted paint.

Underpainting is not an alternative to underdrawing, but usually a second stage. It is generally applied quickly and can be easily removed if unsatisfactory. In this way the tonal balance of the painting can be controlled from the very beginning.

The colors to choose depend upon those to be applied later, but in general, cool colors will complement warmer final layers. The early Italian and Renaissance artists painted warm skin tones over green, blue, or even purple underpainting. Creamy pink or yellowish flesh colors painted as glazes of thin scumbles over such colors acquire a rich, glowing appearance, while the cool greens of foliage are often more forceful if small touches of a warm brown or reddish underpainting are allowed to show through.

As in underdrawing done with a brush, it is most convenient to use the faster-drying colors such as cobalt blue, raw umber, or terre verte, as the underpainting must be dry before further colors are laid. You will have a wider choice of colors if you use acrylic paints (thinned with water), which are very useful in this context, as they will dry within half an hour.

3 In the finished picture very little of the underpainting is visible since great care has been taken to "tidy up" the painting. The main benefit was to allow fluid brush strokes, which help to keep the picture alive. Small, intricate subjects like this can very easily become overworked and tired looking.

WET INTO WET

This technique involves applying colors over and into one another while still wet, and it gives a quite different impression from working wet on dry (see page 41). Because each new brush stroke mixes to some extent with those below or adjacent to it, the results are softer, with forms and colors merging into one another without hard boundaries. Monet (1840–1926) exploited such effects in his rapidly executed outdoor landscapes, often deliberately mixing his colors on the canvas surface by streaking one over another.

Wet into wet is the essence of the *alla prima* approach (see pages 34–35), because the entire painting is done in one session, but the technique can be used for a small part of a painting also. Sky, water, parts of the clothing or face in a portrait, indeed any area where a soft, blended effect is needed, could be painted in this way, while the remainder is built up wet on dry.

Painting wet into wet requires a sure hand and no hesitation; too much reworking will destroy your brushwork, and may result in overmixed, and hence muddy, colors. If the painting begins to look messy and lose its clarity the best course is to scrape it down and start again.

TREES BY THE RIVER by William Garfit RBA

To create the appearance of the treetops blending softly into the sky, the artist has worked wet into wet. Try this method for yourself – you will find it gives a more realistic effect than painting over a dry layer of pigment.

WET ON DRY

If you are completing a painting over a series of sessions you will probably find that you are painting wet on dry whether you planned it or not. Some artists, however, take a more methodical approach and deliberately allow each layer to dry before adding the next, perhaps in order to build up by means of glazing or scumbling.

In pre-Impressionist days, virtually all oil paintings were built up in layers in this way, beginning with an underpainting that established the drawing and tonal structure. It is not a technique for recording quick impressions, but is highly suitable for more complex compositions where there are many different elements, as it gives a higher degree of control over the paint than wet into wet.

It is important to think of each layer as the prelude to the next, and to build up gradually to achieve the contrasts between light and dark areas that will give depth to the painting. The usual method of working – but not the only one – is from dark to light, keeping the paint thin in the initial stages and reserving the thicker highlights until last.

SURVIVORS by Stephen Crowther

Sharp, clear edges like these would be difficult if not impossible to achieve by working wet into wet.

41

FAT OVER LEAN

Paint that has a high percentage of oil is described as "fat," and may be straight from the tube or mixed with extra oil. "Lean" paint is that which has been thinned with turpentine or white spirit only.

The golden rule in oil painting is to paint fat over lean, and there are good reasons for this. The drying oils used both in the manufacture of the paint and as a medium do not evaporate. They simply dry and harden on exposure to air, but this takes a long time (six months to a year to become completely dry). During this process the paint surface shrinks a little. If lean paint has been applied over oily paint the top layer will dry before the lower one has finished shrinking, and this can cause the hardened lean paint to crack and even flake off.

So for any painting built up of several layers the oil content should progressively increase. Any initial underpainting should be done with thinned paints, preferably the low oil ones such as cobalt blue, terre verte, lemon yellow, and flake white. Some tube colors, such as burnt umber and Payne's gray are exceptionally rich in oil and remain fat even when diluted. The next layer can be mixed with a little linseed oil or other medium, while the final ones can be as thick as you like.

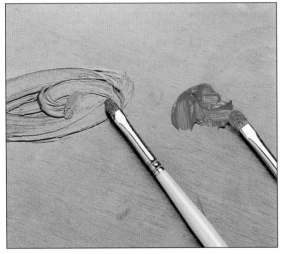

The blue paint on the left is lean, as it has been well diluted with turpentine. The red paint, straight from the tube, has a much more substantial texture.

The painting on page 43 shows a mixture of different paint thicknesses. The blue tabletop consists of quite lean paint while parts of the bottles have been built up with increasingly oily paint.

SPECIAL PAINTING TECHNIQUES

As has been mentioned before, there are many different ways of applying oil paint to create particular effects. Some of these are used almost unconsciously, when the painting seems to demand a particular approach, while others are the result of careful planning.

SCUMBLING

Scumbling falls into the first category of special painting techniques. Scumbling involves applying an uneven layer of paint over a dry, thin, relatively oil-free underpainting so that the first color shows through to some extent. In skillful hands scumbling can create some of the most magical effects in a painting, giving a veil-like impression rather like a filmy fabric placed over a matte one. It is an excellent way of modifying color without sacrificing liveliness, and indeed the scumbled layer itself can be modified by the underpainting so long as this had been planned in advance. For example, you might use a flat, dark red underpainting as a basis for scumbling in lighter red, pink, or even a contrasting color. In addition, the surface texture of the paint is more evocative than flat color, and may well carry the illusion of its subject more effectively.

Dark colors can be scumbled over light ones, but the method is usually more successful with light used over dark. One way to apply a scumble is to load a wide, flat bristle brush with diluted paint, squeeze it to expel as much moisture as possible and then lightly drag it over the surface to produce a very thin film of paint. Thick, undiluted paint is often applied in a circular motion with a well-loaded round bristle brush held perpendicularly. Alternatively a fairly wide flat hog carrying thick paint can be dragged nearly flat to the surface leaving a flecked, broken layer of paint. A round hog or fan dabbed over the surface will create a stippled effect.

Scumbles can also be applied with the fingers, the side of the palm, a rag, a sponge, or a palette knife. The coarser the texture of the canvas the more effective is the scumble because the paint is deposited mainly on the top of the weave. Experimenting with different thicknesses of paint, different surfaces, and different implements held in a variety of ways will give you an idea of the many effects that can be achieved.

1 Pale blue sky has been painted previously and allowed to dry. Clouds are now being built up by scumbling with a rag, using a gentle rocking motion of the finger.

2 Scumbling with a brush leaves bristle marks between which the underlying layer is visible. The method allows soft merging of color with imperceptible gradations.

SCUMBLING (CONTINUED)

In this painting the artist started with a flat underpainting in acrylic, which dries very quickly. Generally a light scumble over a dark color gives the best results. The paint should be fairly dry and applied thinly in gradual stages. Here paint is scumbled gently with the finger. Scumbling is one way to create broken color effects (see pages 32–33).

IMPRINTING

Sometimes you may find that the paint texture provided by brushes or painting knives falls short of your expressive needs. Or you may simply want to experiment with other methods. The slow-drying nature of oil paint, together with its plasticity, enables it to be re-textured on the support itself by pressing a variety of materials or objects into it and then removing them to leave imprints. Almost anything can be used for this method – objects with holes (slotted spoons), grooves (forks), serrated edges (saw blades), or any open structures tend to leave the most satisfactory marks. The thickness of the paint, the pressure you apply, and other factors will affect the texture and quality of the imprint, so try out different effects. Experimentation is essential before committing yourself to part of an actual painting.

This technique is perhaps most relevant to nonrepresentational painting, but it has been used successfully by a number of contemporary artists to create exciting textures where the surface quality of the paint is of paramount importance.

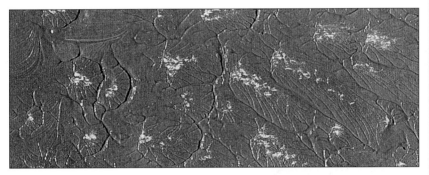

ABOVE: *This pitted and veined pattern has been formed by pressing a teaspoon into wet paint and slightly twisting it.*

RIGHT: *Here green paint has been dabbed with crumpled foil so that a faint image of yellow ground shows through. The streaks are made by the sgraffito technique (see pages 48–49).*

SGRAFFITO

The name sgraffito comes from the Italian *graffiare*, to scratch. This technique involves scoring into the paint after it has been applied to the support. Using any rigid instrument such as a paintbrush handle, a knife, fork, or even a comb, the surface layer of wet paint is scratched to reveal either the ground color or a layer of dry color beneath. Lines of any thickness can be drawn into the paint, and the separate layers of color chosen to contrast or complement each other. Dark brown paint, for example, could be scored to reveal a pale blue, or a dark green to reveal a brighter, lighter one beneath.

Scoring is often used as an accurate way to depict hair, creases in skin, and marks on flat surfaces such as walls or pavements. Rembrandt (1606–1669)

used the technique extensively, scribbling into thick, wet paint with a brush handle to pick out individual hairs in a sitter's moustache or the pattern of lace on a collar. Shaded areas can be developed by hatching with the scorer to reveal dark under-painting. Wavelets on the sea, patches of light sky within foliage, or flashes and sparks in a fire can all be suggested in this way.

The quality of line depends on the thickness of the paint and to what extent it has dried. Even when thoroughly dry, paint can be scratched into as long as a really sharp point is used. In this case the scored lines will be white, as all the layers of paint will be removed, but this can be effective for some subjects. It is best to restrict scratching into dry paint to rigid boards, however, as it might damage canvas.

1 The background color of the wooden tabletop is applied in fairly thick paint. The pattern of the wood grain will be scraped into this paint at a later stage. The ground color is dark brown, and it is this that will appear as the paint is scratched off.

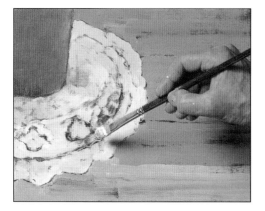

3 The artist uses a painting knife to "draw" in the pattern of the wood grain.

2 In this photograph the doily is being painted white prior to sgraffito.

5 It is also an excellent method for obtaining thin lines in thick paint that would become unmanageable if yet more paint were added. Here lines are inscribed with the "wrong" end of a paintbrush.

4 Knots in the wood can be described admirably by this technique.

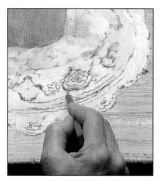

6 The complex pattern of the doily is drawn into the still-wet paint with a pencil. Like the paintbrush handle used earlier, this scrapes the paint aside, but it also leaves its own mark, the brown ground only showing in the regions where it was left unpainted.

IMPASTO

The term impasto describes paint that has been applied thickly enough to retain the marks and ridges left by the brush or painting knife. The ability to build up oil paint is for many people one of its main attractions. The picture surface can acquire a three-dimensional quality that can be used to model form and even mimic the texture of the subject. Turner (1775–1851) built up layers of paint in the pale areas of his paintings, such as clouds and sun, and some of Rembrandt's portraits are almost like relief sculptures.

Thickly applied paint is often used in conjunction with glazing. A dark glaze over a light-colored impasto will cling to the grooves and pits, emphasizing the brushwork. This can be an effective way of depicting texture; for example,

rough stone or wood.

The paint can be applied with a brush or painting knife for impasto work, or it can even be squeezed out straight from the tube. Some makes of paint are particularly oily, in which case excess oil should be absorbed by blotting paper or the brush marks may become blurred. If the paint is too thick a little linseed oil can be added. There are also mediums specially made for impasto work, which act as extenders, bulking out the paint. For anyone working on a large scale these are very helpful, as they can halve your paint costs. They also help the paint to retain the marks of the brush and speed the drying process, which is an important consideration when more layers of paint are to be added.

THE ARTIST'S FATHER by George Rowlett

This artist likes thick paint, and often applies it with knives and his fingers as well as brushes. In this powerful yet sensitive portrait he has allowed the thick, juicy color to dribble down the canvas in places, and has used it throughout in an inventive and expressive way.

1 So far only fairly thin paint has been used. The brushwork is rather monotonous and the picture lacks vitality, so the artist decides to introduce some eye-catching accents.

3 Some yellow ocher "pushed" into the white suggests churned-up sand, while the gray provides shadows below the tops of the breakers. Finally a thin sable brush was used to lay cadmium red impasto as a foreground accent.

2 Thick, unmixed white paint is dabbed in place to represent foaming breakers.

4 The whipped cream quality of the impasto is clearly seen in this photograph. It will not change as it dries – one of the unique characteristics of oil paint.

TONKING

A painting will often reach a stage when it becomes unworkable because there is too much paint on the surface. Any new color simply mixes with that below, creating unpleasant muddy mixtures as well as disturbing previous brushwork. When this happens, the excess can be removed by "tonking," a method named after Henry Tonks, a former professor of painting at the Slade School of Art in London. A sheet of absorbent paper such as newspaper or paper towel is placed over the overloaded area – or the whole painting – gently rubbed with the palm of the hand and then carefully peeled off. This carries off the top layer of paint, leaving a thinned-out version of the original, with softer outlines, which serves as an ideal underpainting over which to continue.

Tonking is particularly useful in portraiture because it eliminates details while leaving the main structure of the head firmly established. It is usually details, particularly within the eyes and mouth which, even if only slightly misplaced, will destroy the likeness in a portrait. These also tend to become heavily loaded with paint, as there is a tendency to put on layer after layer in the attempt to get them right. Sometimes the action of tonking produces a passage which needs little or no further painting.

1 A common mistake is to build up the paint too thickly in the early stages of painting. It is virtually impossible to continue working over a layer of impasto this thick.

2 Newspaper or any other absorbent paper is carefully laid over the part of the painting to be tonked, and is rubbed firmly with the palm of the hand to ensure that the upper layers of paint adhere to it. The paper is slowly peeled off the painting, bringing the paint with it.

3 After tonking only a thin layer of paint remains, with brush marks smoothed away and details eliminated. This is an ideal surface for further working. Tonking can be performed as often as you like during the course of painting.

GLAZING

A glaze is a thin layer of transparent paint laid over a dry layer that can be either thick or thin. Since the lower layer is visible through the glaze, the effect is quite different from anything that can be achieved with opaque paint.

The Renaissance painters achieved wonderfully luminous reds and blues by building up successive layers of ever-richer color, using little or no opaque paint, but glazing over impasto is equally effective. Rembrandt (1606–1669) built up the light areas of his portraits with thick flake white modified by a series of glazes, and Turner created his distant luminous skies by the same method. Rembrandt always used transparent paint for shadow areas, which gave the dark passages a rich glow and an effect of insubstantiality – the eye is unable to judge exactly where the light is coming from.

Since a glaze alters the color of an underlying layer it can serve as a method of color mixing. For example, a transparent ultramarine blue glaze over yellow produces a green, while a glaze of alizarin crimson over blue will make purple.

Before a glaze is applied the previous layer of paint must be dry to the touch. If glazing is to be put on directly over an underpainting, the latter can be done in acrylic paint (which dries in some cases within minutes). Oil glazes, or indeed any oil paint, will lie perfectly well over acrylic, but acrylic cannot be laid over oil.

The best mediums to use for glazing are the modern synthetic ones sold specially for the purpose; ask your art supplier if you are not certain what to buy. Because a high proportion of oil is needed to make the paint transparent, it will simply run down the support or merge with adjacent glazes.

1 Mix the color on your palette, then add an equal quantity of medium. The paint should have a thin but oily consistency. Be careful though not to overthin! Do not dilute the paint with turpentine alone – this makes the color go flat and dull, and sometimes results in a cracked surface. For best results, apply the glaze with a large, flat, soft-haired brush.

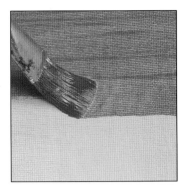

2 Apply the glaze in a thin layer over a light ground. The color appears bright because of light reflecting back off the canvas. Lay the canvas flat to prevent drips and runs.

3 Allow each layer to dry fully before adding more glaze. This example shows how the color underneath glows through the glaze, giving the paint a three-dimensional quality.

DRY BRUSH

The dry brush technique is a method of applying color lightly so that it only partially covers a dry layer of color below. The minimum of paint should be used on the brush, and the brush strokes should be made quickly and with confidence – overworking destroys the effect. Dry brush is most successful when there is already some existing texture, either that of the canvas or that provided by previous brush strokes.

It is a useful method of suggesting texture, for instance, that of weathered rock or long grass, but like all "special" techniques, should never be overdone or treated as a short cut.

WINTER, DERBYSHIRE by Hazel Harrison

Foregrounds are often tricky, but here the problem has been elegantly solved by the assertive painting of the weather-beaten hay. It has been applied swiftly with relatively dry paint on a thin round brush.

1 The artist uses a fan brush to lay a scant overpainting of thick, undiluted paint. The bristles of this type of brush are well splayed and deposit paint in a light covering of fine separate lines.

2 The same technique has been used for the intricate pattern made by the branches of the small tree.

3 Dry brush is most effective when used light over dark. Here you can see how a succession of mostly paler layers are added one over the other.

ALTERNATIVE TECHNIQUES

KNIFE PAINTING

Applying thick paint with knives gives a quite different effect from applying similarly thick paint with brushes. The knife squeezes the paint onto the surface, leaving a series of flat, smooth planes often bordered by ridges or lines where each stroke ends. It is a versatile and expressive method, although initially somewhat trickier than brush painting. The marks can be varied by the direction of the knife, the amount of paint loaded onto it, the degree of pressure applied, and of course the knives themselves.

Painting knives are not the same as palette knives, which are intended only for mixing paint on the palette and for cleaning up. Unlike the latter, they have cranked handles and extremely flexible blades of forged steel. They are made in a wide variety of shapes and sizes from large straight ones to tiny pear-shapes ideal for flicking paint onto the surface.

Knife painting is ideal for the artist who enjoys the sensuous, "hands-on" aspect of mixing and applying thick, creamy paint. However, care must be taken not to build up the paint too thickly; it may crack if it is more than about half a centimeter thick at its maximum.

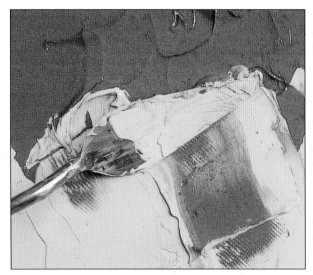

Knife painting needs to be done with confidence and no hesitation, so it is wise to practice before trying out the method on a painting. The effect is quite different from that of brush strokes; notice how the paint is squashed out in ridges at the edges. When one color is laid over another there will be some mixing and streaking of the paint, which can be very effective.

SAN GIORGIO MAGGIORE, VENICE by Jeremy Galton

Knives are often used only for certain parts of a painting, such as final highlights in thick impasto, but in this case the whole picture was built up with knife strokes, giving a lively surface texture. It is a technique well suited to architectural subjects, as considerable precision can be achieved.

DAFYDD WILLIAMS ON THE MOUNTAINS by Kaffyn Williams

Here the artist has worked entirely with painting knives. This technique gives a much harsher effect than impasto applied with a brush, and the pattern of angular slabs and ridges of paint gives additional feeling and drama to the somber subject matter.

59

FINGER PAINTING

Finger painting is perhaps the most natural, and certainly the most direct method of applying paints, and although it has slight connotations of "child art" it has a definite place in serious painting. The fingers are sensitive tools, and are often superior to either brush or palette knife for subtle effects and fine control of paint thickness. Many painters have used the technique, among them Leonardo da Vinci (1452–1519), Titian (c.1487/90–1576), Goya (1746–1828), and Turner (1775–1851). It is said of Titian that he would soften outlines, dab in highlights, accents, and other final touches by using his fingers more than his brush.

The fingers and hand are particularly useful for the rapid application of undiluted paint over large areas, as it can be rubbed well into the canvas fibers to give a greater degree of adherence. Paint can also be smeared off by hand until it is at its desired thickness. When modeling rounded forms, as in portraiture or figure painting, this technique can be invaluable, as it allows you to obtain very smooth gradations of color and tone in which the underlying layer shows through as much or as little as you want it to.

It should be borne in mind, however, that many pigments are toxic, so always clean your hands thoroughly at the end of a painting session. You can also avoid direct contact with the paint altogether by working with a rag wrapped around your fingers or bundled into a suitably shaped wad.

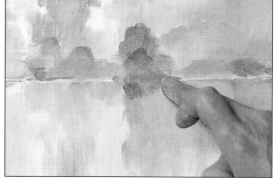

1 A combination of fingers and brushes was used for this painting. Having blocked in the basic features in slightly diluted paint the artist blends them with her finger and then adds further thin layers. She is careful to keep the colors very close in tone so as not to lose the misty atmosphere.

2 Layer upon layer of pale colors are rubbed into one another in the sky area to produce an indefinable and luminous quality. The trees, in contrast, are blended to a lesser degree to retain their pale but distinct outlines.

3 The contours of the distant trees are smudged into the sky so that they appear to recede from the viewer.

4 The water, like the sky, is built up of many thin layers of paint. The thickness of the paint can be very precisely controlled by the finger method, and in this case it becomes both thicker and darker toward the bottom of the picture. The finished picture has a wonderfully atmospheric effect. The picture has been painted in a limited color range and in a high key – that is, only pale color mixtures have been used.

COLLAGE

The first time collage was used in oil painting was in 1912 when Picasso (1881–1973) stuck a piece of oil-cloth onto his canvas to represent a caned chair seat. The Cubist painters, notably Braque (1882–1963), continued to exploit this new concept, adding pieces of newspaper, stamped envelopes, theater tickets, and wallpaper to their paintings. The purpose of sticking real objects to the picture surface was to emphasize the existence of the picture as an object in its own right as opposed to an illusion of reality.

"Found" objects can either be fastened with glue to the virgin canvas or board, or pressed into thick, wet oil paint, which serves as a good adhesive. Sand, pebbles, bits of wood, in fact almost anything can be added to the paint to create special textures, although for any but purely experimental work it is important to

THE SUNBLIND by Juan Gris

Several of the Cubist painters experimented with collage, as they were interested in the relationship of image (or illusion) to object, and the use of real objects such as pieces of wallpaper, theater programs, and tickets emphasized this. In this picture newspaper and wallpaper were combined with oil paint. Some textures have been built up by stippling and spattering.

consider the permanence of the additions. Paper, for example, tends to yellow quickly, and certain organic materials can rot or crumble in time.

Collage can also be used as a stage in painting rather than an end in itself; the artist will sometimes decide on his next step by painting new areas on paper and temporarily sticking them to the canvas. This is a helpful method for working out the exact placing of figures in a landscape, for example. The collaged figures can be moved around, changed in color, size, or posture until the artist has found what he or she wants. The collage is then removed and the painting proceeds as usual.

CAPILIERA ROOFTOPS by Barbara Rae

Overlapping planes of smooth and wrinkled paper are dominant in this richly-colored composition. Rae will use almost any materials to construct her collages provided they are not prone to deterioration. As shown in the detail on the right, the shapes of the chimneys are cut out of paper, forming sharp contours that contrast with other, softer edges. Not all paper is suitable for collage; the colors of tissue paper, for example, fade very quickly.

POINTILLISM

Pointillism is the technique of covering the whole canvas with tiny dabs or points of color laid side by side, but not overlapping, so that when viewed from a distance they merge together to create effects of color and tone. Evolving from the Impressionists' use of broken color, the technique was pioneered by Georges Seurat (1859–1891), who preferred to use the term divisionism. Seurat was fascinated by color theory, and greatly influenced by the new scientific discoveries about the properties of light and color made by Chevreul and

Rood, who had shown that different colors when lying next to each other will mix in the eye of the viewer. The principle of optical mixing is made use of in both color television and color printing – an entire picture is composed of countless dots of three primary colors.

Seurat not only created secondary and tertiary colors in this way but also believed he could enhance the apparent brightness of one color by placing its complementary next to it and vice versa – another of Chevreul's theories.

Wonderful as many of Seurat's paintings are, Pointillism in its pure form is a very limited painting technique, as several other artists who took up the idea quickly discovered. Camille Pissarro (1830–1903), Paul Signac (1863–1935), and Henri-Edmond Cross (1856–1910) were all enthusiastic about it, but soon began to modify it by enlarging the dabs of paint so that they would contribute toward the composition rather than merging into a single image.

RIGHT: ELY CATHEDRAL by Arthur Maderson

The major part of the overpainting is made up of stabs of relatively dry paint dragged onto the surface, allowing the previous statement to show through. The artist has used fairly pure colors that mix optically when viewed at a distance, and parts of the painting are very close to Seurat's own Pointillism.

LEFT: THE CAN-CAN by Georges Seurat

In this painting the separate dots of pure color have resulted in an overall subdued tint. This may be at least in part because of fading; Seurat's contemporaries began to notice a dulling of the colors soon after his pictures were finished. The minute size of each brush stroke gives a good idea of how slow and laborious the method must have been. It is hardly surprising that later artists modified it, but Pointillism has nevertheless been extremely influential.

BRUSH TECHNIQUES

Because oil paint has a thick buttery consistency (if not too diluted) it is the perfect medium with which to exploit the marks of the brush. Since the paint does not change as it hardens and dries, brush strokes remain exactly as they were when first applied, with every bristle mark clearly visible, providing a visual history of the painter's manner of working.

Paint can be applied rapidly or slowly and methodically; the brush marks can all run in the same direction; they can be used directionally to describe a shape or form; or they can swirl around the picture, as in van Gogh's paintings. Whatever form it takes, brushwork provides the texture on the painted surface that is an integral part of the picture – indeed in many cases a painting almost is its brushwork.

Obviously there is a direct relationship between the marks and the brushes chosen. These are available in a variety of shapes, as shown here, and it is worth spending time experimenting with all of them to discover their possibilities. Try them with different paint consistencies and on different supports. Make rapid swept strokes and then slower ones; dab them lightly, at different angles and vertically; experiment with holding a brush in different ways or twirling it during its stroke. It may take

Flats make distinctive square or rectangular marks, much exploited by the Impressionists.

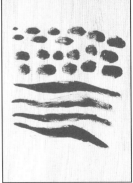

Filberts are extremely versatile brushes. They can leave rounded dabs of paint or be twisted during a stroke to create marks of varying thickness.

Rounds, when held vertically, are ideal for stippling. They can also deliver long, continuous strokes.

some time to discover your painting "handwriting," but remember that brushwork is not just an exercise or a way of embellishing a picture, it is a means to express yourself and your personal perception of the subject.

RUE VIVIANI by Peter Graham

The artist began by making linear strokes with medium-sized synthetic flats and hog filberts. Large areas were then rapidly blocked in with large flat bristle brushes, and the subsequent free-flowing brush marks were made with large rounds and filberts. The latter were also used for the more intricate work, and the dappling of sunlight on the tree trunks and figures (left) was added with round sable and synthetic brushes. The effect is one of lively spontaneity.

VARIOUS BRUSHSTROKES

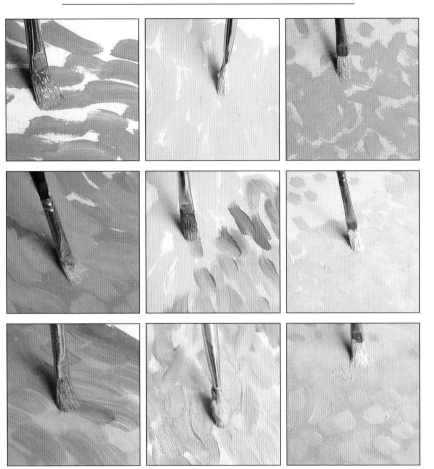

FLUID STROKES
Here the artist uses a No. 4 flat brush to apply fluid, curving strokes. Light and dark tones are juxtaposed, without blending, to build up a mosaic of color. The rhythmical force of these strokes brings to mind the paintings of van Gogh.

SHORT STROKES
Claude Monet was perhaps the greatest exponent of Impressionism: he covered his canvases with tiny, irregular strokes like these, color over color.

STIPPLED STROKES
The gentle, shimmering quality of Alfred Sisley's paintings derives from his use of pale, translucent colors, applied with small stippled strokes with the end of the brush. Notice how the pale, creamy ground shows through in places.

ABOVE: LISMORE FÊTE by Arthur Maderson

All eyes are turned toward a source of entertainment beyond the edge of the frame, yet such is the richness of the brushwork, color, and texture on the picture surface that our eyes remain held by it. Indeed, although the figures are beautifully observed and stated, the painting has a powerful physical presence of its own which has less to do with the subject than the way it is treated.

RIGHT: MOTHER-IN-LAW IN BLUE HAT by Naomi Alexander

The brushwork here makes an obvious contribution to the character of the painting, with individual bristle marks clearly visible, criss-crossing over each other. The whole picture has been built up from very thin layers of paint streaked or scumbled over previously dried layers.

COLOR EFFECTS

As you gradually develop the range of colors in a painting, you will find that the appearance of individual colors seems to change each time you introduce a new element. Colors are relative; they interact and react to one another on the working surface. Although pigments are standardized to create reliable color values, the visual qualities of any color are influenced by the context in which it is seen.

Color theories that were devised during the 19th century were an attempt to give color analysis a scientific basis, so that using color could be a more controlled and predictable exercise.

DISCORDANT COLORS

Some color relationships are naturally discordant – the colors compete or clash with each other, setting up visual vibrations. Discordant colors can create very exciting effects, and such color vibrations are exploited by some contemporary artists. A visual "screaming" effect can be created by juxtaposing two complementary colors. This relationship would normally be harmonious, but by marginally adjusting the tonal order, one can make the relationship discordant. If, for example, blue and orange were laid side by side, a blue-orange discord would be created by making the blue fractionally lighter than the orange. Vibrations and discords are created more dramatically when the pairs of colors involved are complementaries, or nearly complementary, and when they are intense and of the same value. These effects are set up along the edges of the color areas and can be maximized by the creation of many color boundaries.

Any two colors can be made to clash either by making the tonal values equal or by creating an inversion of the natural tonal order of the hues. You will find that some pairs of colors will be more difficult than others. Of the complementary pairs violet and yellow will probably cause the most difficulty. Remember that violet must be made as light or even lighter than yellow. It will therefore appear almost white and will seem to have lost its hue, but the addition of white does not actually alter the hue of a color.

You may wonder why anyone would want to create color discords, but these startling effects can be very useful and are often exploited in both commercial advertising and painting.

USING A LIMITED PALETTE

It is advisable to start with a small palette such as this so that you get to know the mixtures you can – and cannot – achieve. Other colors can be purchased later if needed.

In any case too wide a color range can diminish a painting. Both Turner (1775–1851) and Monet (1840–1926) created subtle harmonies by using a range of blues and blue-grays with occasional touches of yellow for contrast. This bias toward one dominating hue is called a color key, and can be identified in the majority of paintings.

You an learn a great deal by deliberately restricting your palette, so if a subject strikes you as being predominantly green, blue, or brown, try to stay within that range of colors again and again in different mixtures.

The arrangement of paints on your palette is purely personal, but be consistent so that you can always quickly find the color you want. The dark colors all look rather similar, so knowing their positions will prevent you from picking the wrong one and ruining a mixture. With experience you will get to know the relative quantities to squeeze out of the tubes so that wastage is kept to a minimum. The colors on this palette are, from right to left: titanium white, French ultramarine, cobalt blue, viridian, lemon yellow, cadmium yellow, yellow ocher, burnt umber, cadmium red, alizarin crimson, and Payne's gray. The same colors, minus the white, are shown in the upper photograph.

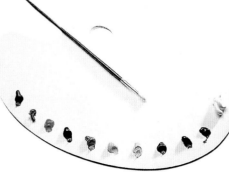

COLOR THEMES

Most paintings can be seen as falling into one of three broad categories in terms of color scheme: a general impression of harmony derived from a range of related or similar colors; deliberate contrast formed by exploiting obviously differing color characteristics, such as complementary

THE SUMMER READ by Timothy Easton

The painting's natural setting contributes to a harmonious effect, but the individual colors represent the entire spectrum and form a complex color harmony. There are direct, linking relationships – yellow to green, green to blue, blue to purple – and also direct opposites. The latter is most obvious in the complementary yellow and purple contrast, but tiny pink and red accents also complement the greens.

or warm/cool contrasts; or a "multi-colored" effect, in which the color relationships are apparently much more random, due to many variations of local color in the subject and further modifications created by the pattern of light and shade.

When you select or set up a subject for painting, you may initially be attracted by a harmonious or complementary scheme inherent in the subject, or see the possibility of arranging the components in such a way by choosing particular props and accessories. No scheme has to be exclusive, however. For example, if you are working with related colors, you may wish to include small accents of contrasting color that will give the picture a lift without disrupting the overall harmony. If you are using complementaries or warm/cool contrast, you may be spreading the contrasting elements fairly evenly throughout the picture, or you might arrange them in a way that makes one kind of color dominate a particular area of the picture, with the contrast more broadly stated elsewhere.

Where color sensations are more complex and varied, you can take one of two approaches. You can deal with them in the broadest possible way by trying to find equivalents for all the colors and tones, or you can approach the subject more selectively, revising the key of the hues and tones in order to organize relationships and oppositions more deliberately.

The selection of paint or pastel colors that you start with directly controls whether you are able to match the subject's given color range. As explained in the first section of the book, particular red and blue pigments produce brown when mixed, not violet or purple. Particular blues and yellows in combination produce certain types of green. The fundamental character of that mixed color is not going to change whatever you do with it, so you need to begin with a palette of colors that can provide sufficient variation.

However, you can also manipulate the color relationships to some extent within the image to enhance or subdue certain effects and interactions. The ways of doing this mainly depend on varying the balance between like and unlike color characteristics – intense, pure hues versus muted and neutral colors; light against dark tones; complementary contrast; oppositions of warm and cool color. In addition, you can use the paint texture to help you vary visual effects – contrasting the flatness and density of opaque colors with the luminous and variable surface qualities of transparent colors, using techniques of layering the picture surface and building up complex patterns of broken color.

LANDSCAPE GREENS

In the far distance, the greens are blued and neutralized.

Blue-greens create depth at the center of the picture, drawing the viewer into the townscape.

Bright mid-toned greens convey sunlight playing on the outer branches of the massed foliage.

Cool blue-purple shadows emphasize the relatively warm qualities of the yellow-greens.

DELL PUIG MARIA by Olwen Tarrant

The artist achieves the effect of brilliant sunshine by using a predominance of yellow-greens in the foreground. Their brightness matches that of the reflected light in the townscape behind, while in the distance all the colors are muted. The composition is unified by many subtle links and contrasts between warm and cool color variations.

High-key greens and yellows in the foreground hold their position against the brightly lit middle ground.

USING COLOR TO CONVEY TRANSLUCENCY

A material that is translucent but not fully transparent, such as smoked glass or thin fabric, combines some of the the visual effects of glass or metal – it has a color of its own, it reflects from its surface and also transmits colors and tones. But translucency commonly has a slightly hazy effect, without the powerful contrasts seen in reflective and transparent materials, and the gradations of color and tone are less abrupt.

The key is to bring everything to the surface – interpret the shapes and colors as a kind of jigsaw of inter-locking elements rather than receding layers. You need to identify very subtle color relationships where background colors are merged with the colors and tones of the intervening material and the play of light acting upon it. However, you may be able to employ techniques of layering your paint surface to handle some visual effects. Scumbling, a thin veil of semi-opaque color brushed lightly over underlying layers, has exactly the subtle, gauzy effect of see-through fabric. Drybrushing, a more emphatic, broken-color effect, can also work well.

But remember that the form of the object or piece of fabric affects the character of underlying shapes – think how the folds in a fine muslin curtain, for example, can distort the lines of a window frame behind. You cannot make a formalized picture of what lies behind and then scumble the "veiling" over the top, however, tempting such a straightforward solution may seem.

EASTERN VIEW by Timothy Easton

The exact quality of the translucent drapes is conveyed through subtle color variations within a narrow tonal range and drybrushed textures that create a veiled effect. These elements are beautifully integrated with the distorted patterning of direct and reflected light through the window.

75

MIXED MEDIA

This term is most often found in the context of "works on paper," which may be mixtures of watercolor with gouache, pastel, pencils, wax crayons and so on, but other media can also be used in combination with oil paints. It can be very liberating not to be bound by one medium, and is sometimes a way to save a less than successful painting.

As is explained in the fat over lean section (pages 42–43), oily pigments can be applied over less oily ones. Thus underpainting in watercolor, gouache, and particularly acrylic forms a very good base for overpainting in oil.

The mix of textures provided by the use of different media can be highly expressive. Fast-drying acrylic paints can be applied both thinly like watercolor, or thickly like oils, and are frequently used nowadays to lay the first few stages of a painting.

You cannot paint with acrylic over oil, as the paint does not adhere, but oil, once dry, can be worked over with both soft pastel and oil pastel, and drawn into and over with pencils. Such techniques can produce intriguing broken textures, rather like dry brush painting, and also provide a means of sharpening up and redefining edges and small details. If pastels are used, the picture should be mounted under glass for protection, so if you plan a mixed-media approach it may be best to use a paper support.

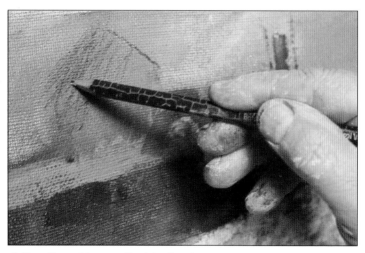

1 Pencil combines well with oil paint, and here the artist is using one to redefine forms and to provide a variety of textures. Much of the penciling will remain visible in the final picture.

2 Oil pastel can be dabbed and stippled over oil paint, and in this case is ideal for describing the dancing light on the water.

3 The graphic quality of the pencil, the heavy texture of the canvas, the large swathes of oil paint, and the dabs of oil pastel complement one another beautifully. It is worth mentioning that this exciting painting was derived from a rather dull photograph; the inventive use of media minimizes the temptation of direct copying and encourages the artist toward a personal means of expression.

OIL GLAZE OVER ACRYLIC

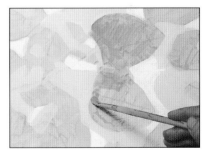

1 Using acrylic paint, the leaves are reduced to two tones of green, with the paint used thinly, and the brush strokes suggesting the visible skeleton of the leaves.

2 An oil glaze made from a mixture of sap green and cadmium yellow thinned with glazing medium is laid over the dry underpainting, modifying the darker tones.

MAKING CHANGES

One of the advantages of working in oils is that corrections can be made easily either to the whole painting or to small passages.

When painting *alla prima*, wet paint can simply be scraped off with a palette knife. This may leave a ghost of the previous image, which can either be retained to act as a guide for the fresh attempt or removed with white spirit on a rag. If a painting becomes unworkable because it is overloaded with paint, the top layer can be lifted off with absorbent paper (see tonking on pages 52–53).

In the case of a painting that is to be built up of a number of layers, you can facilitate later corrections by rubbing a little linseed oil (or whatever medium us being used) into the previous dry layer before adding more color. This is called "oiling out," and it not only assists the application

of wet paint, but also makes it easier to remove if you need to.

Thick impasto takes at least several weeks to dry, so within this period it can still be scraped off if necessary. However, this becomes increasingly difficult as it begins to dry, and may necessitate using sharp knives or razor blades. It is always best to paint thin layers first with as little oil as possible (see fat over lean pages 42–43), leaving thick impasto to the very end when it is less likely to need alteration.

An area of thin, dried paint that requires correction can simply be overpainted, but existing paintwork can be very distracting if small modifications are being attempted. It may be better to either sandpaper down the offending area, which will remove at least some of the paint, or paint a new ground over this patch and start again.

1 Much of the paintwork at the lower left of this picture is unsatisfactory and has become thick and unworkable. It is consequently removed, initially by scraping off with a small painting knife.

2 Scraping back leaves a ghost of the original image that can often form a helpful base on which to rework.

3 In this case, however, scraped-back paint is completely removed with a rag dipped in white spirit.

5 Dry paint can be removed with sandpaper as long as it is not too thick.

4 The area is now reworked. Corrections such as these are easy to make when the paint is still wet.

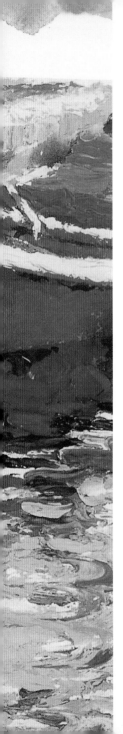

COLOR AND COMPOSITION

Man's first experiments with color are recorded in the paleolithic cave paintings of France and Spain. The paints used were naturally occurring earth colors, which gave various shades of red, yellow, and black. Greens and blues were not found. Artists today have access to an enormous range of colors in all the media, many of which have only become available in the last thirty years, and art historians can sometimes date paintings very precisely by studying the colors used by the artist. Painting is not just about manual dexterity or an extensive knowledge of paints and pigments, or the chemical composition of grounds and binders. It is about looking, learning to see, and making something of what we see. Only when you start to paint do you realize how little you have seen before.

COMPOSITION

CHOOSING A SUBJECT

For many beginners the choice of subject presents an appalling problem – they just cannot think of anything to paint. Of course the answer is that anything and everything is fair game for the artist. Just look around you as you read this and you will see any number of "pictures": the texture of a table; the view glimpsed through the window; the figure of a friend leaning against the door jamb engrossed in a conversation; a bowl of fruit; or wilting flowers, their petals scattered on the table. Can't think of anything to paint indeed!

Many painters seem to think that some subjects are more legitimate than others, but this is really not so. Any subject can be the basis of a painting, but the choice must depend on your interests and on the opportunities available to you. The best idea is to start with subjects close at hand.

Still life provides the painter with wonderful opportunities for exploring ideas about color, composition, and painting. The subjects are close at hand and the choice is almost limitless. It is also the only subject that is entirely under your control. It is not restricted by schedules, and you can continue to work on a subject over a period of time – unless, of course, you have included fruit or vegetables which may rot. When choosing the objects, go for themes, select particular colors or contrasting shapes and textures, and don't forget that you can play with the lighting.

Interiors are an excellent subject, setting you the problem of creating an

The artist has found a subject in the view through the studio doorway and used oil paint, thinly diluted with turpentine, to make a rapid sketch of the view. He handled the paint freely, laying in the broad outlines of the subject.

illusion of space and coping with the perspective. Further interest is added if the room is illuminated from outside, so that the enclosed intimate feeling of an interior space is enhanced by glimpses of a contrasting exterior.

USING REFERENCE MATERIAL

Reference material is very important for most artists. Never leave home without a sketchbook and always have one lying open at home, with a drawing implement close at hand. The journey to work, the office, lunch in the park, all these occasions provide you with information for your sketch-book, and these sketches can be incorporated and collated to create interesting pictures. Other reference material to jog the visual imagination and act as a catalyst to your creativity includes newspaper pictures, pages torn from magazines, and, of course, your own photographs. The subject of photographs is a difficult one – many people disapprove of using photographs as the basis of paintings. What they are really objecting to is the fact that the camera has been allowed to do the selecting and, because selection is one of the artist's most important contributions, there is a risk that paintings from photographs will be

dull, lifeless copies of the photograph. Nevertheless, it should be borne in mind that the camera does to some extent distort reality. Some of these fortuitous distortions have been taken up and exploited by artists such

Firmly bound sketchbooks are used a great deal by artists who build up studio paintings from sketched notes made elsewhere, especially outdoors.

as Degas and, especially, Walter Sickert (1860–1942). Again, as long as you are aware of what is happening, you can decide what you will use and can treat the material in the photograph in your own way.

THE GEOMETRY OF A PICTURE

Since ancient times artists have considered the geometrical proportions of their compositions. The artists of Ancient Egypt divided the walls on which they were going to paint into a network of verticals and horizontals, and along these they arranged the elements of their compositions in such a way as to create a harmonious effect. Artists have evolved various formulas to help them achieve stability and coherence. One of these is the Golden Section, one of the most important of the systems with which artists sought to codify these particularly pleasing proportions. It is defined as a line that is divided in such a way that the smaller part is to the larger part as

All paintings can be analyzed in terms of their underlying geometry. The painting (far left) has a strong vertical stress, whereas the picture (left) has a dominant horizontality balanced by a vertical. (Middle, far left) the composition has a strong diagonal stress, whereas that of the picture (middle left) is based on a triangle. (Bottom, far left) we see a "busy," all-over pattern and (bottom left), we see "empty" areas contrasted with busy ones.

the larger part is to the whole. It is used to divide lines and create shapes that are aesthetically harmonious. In practice it works out at about 1:1.618, and it is surprising how often this proportion occurs in both art and nature. The Golden Section has been known since the time of the Greek mathematician Euclid, and was particularly popular in the Renaissance. The proportions of this formula can be identified in many paintings of the fifteenth century and ever since.

THE GOLDEN SECTION

Painters of the Renaissance usually planned the composition of a painting on a geometric grid structure based on a triangle. A common compositional device which is still much used, as are circles and rectangles.

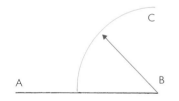

1 Divide line AB into two sections of equal length.

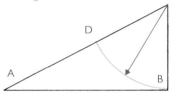

4 With the compass on C, draw an arc from B to cut $\overline{\text{AC}}$ at point D.

2 Put the point of the compass on B and draw an arc from the midpoint of the line to point C, at right angles to $\overline{\text{AB}}$.

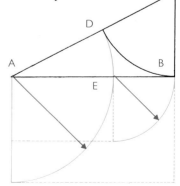

3 Join C to points A and B. This forms a right triangle.

5 With the compass on A, draw an arc from B to cut $\overline{\text{AB}}$ at point E. In proportion, $\overline{\text{EB}}$ is to $\overline{\text{AE}}$ as $\overline{\text{AE}}$ is to $\overline{\text{AB}}$. A rectangle can now be drawn according to the Golden Section.

SHAPE AND SIZE

This may seem trivial, but in fact both shape and size have an important part to play in the composition and treatment of a painting. When you are constructing a picture don't forget to include the shape and size of your support in your calculations. Different shapes suggest different emotions and moods – a square will convey a sense of stability and compact solidity, whereas a long narrow rectangle will suggest calm. Pictures have been painted within many shapes but they are usually rectangular.

The size of the support is important. Think of a painting that you knew well from reproductions and were quite shocked to come across in a gallery because it was either so much larger or so much smaller than you imagined. When choosing the scale for a painting or drawing, be guided by the demands of the subject and the medium. For instance, pencil is best on quite a small scale; if you attempt anything larger you will set yourself enormous problems. Artists sometimes work on a particular shape and size of canvas for no better reason than that it is the only one available, and the painting then evolves restricted by those parameters, sometimes with unhappy results.

If you buy prepared boards or canvases you are obviously limited by the range of sizes on the market, but if you prepare your own you can choose what suits you. Some painters use ready-processed canvases that come in a limited range of shapes and sizes. This may be habit or laziness, or may be for economic reasons. It is, however, a good idea to try something different periodically – if you habitually work very small try working on a large painting, or vice versa.

PENCIL MEASUREMENTS

You can check both sizes and angles with a pencil held out in front of the subject. For size comparison, be sure to hold the pencil with your arm completely straight, and to remain in the same position for each measurement. When checking angles, be careful to keep the pencil at the same angle when you bring it down to the paper to mark in your line.

DEFINING THE COMPOSITION

The word "composition" has a slightly alarming ring to it – it sounds as though it might be an intellectual exercise quite beyond the capabilities of the ordinary person. This really is not so: composing a painting is mainly a question of selecting, arranging and rearranging, just as you might do when deciding on the decor for a room or when taking a photograph. A large, complex painting with numerous people and objects in it does, of course, need some thought, otherwise there may be too much activity in one part of the picture and not enough in another. But even here, it is less a matter of following a prescribed set of rules than of working out the balance of the various shapes, as in the case of planning a room – no one would put all the furniture crowded together on one side and leave the rest empty.

A "good composition" is one in which there is no jarring note, the colors and shapes are well balanced, and the picture as a whole seems to sit easily within its frame or outer borders. Even a simple head-and-shoulders portrait is composed, and a vital part of composition is selection – what you put in and what you leave out. In the case of a portrait you will need to establish whether the person should be seated, and if so on what, whether you want to include the chair, whether you want the hands to form part of the composition, and whether you want to use something in the background, for example part of a window frame, to balance the figure.

If you are painting a landscape you may think composition is not involved,

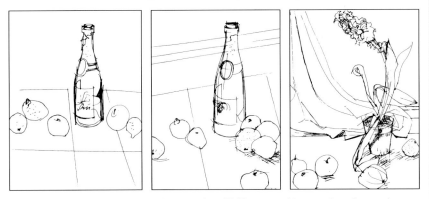

These drawings show the different elements of a still life arranged in a variety of ways. A symmetrical arrangement (far left) tends to be monotonous, but the arrangement, with the flat plane of the table angled away from the eye and a more varied grouping of the fruit (middle), has more visual interest. The drawing of the flower and fruit with draperies (right) provides more linear contrasts and a busier background.

that you are just painting what you see, but you will have chosen a particular view, just as you would when taking a photograph, and in choosing it you will have gone at least some way toward composing it. You may then find that you want to exaggerate or rearrange some feature in the foreground, such as a rock or a tree, to provide extra interest, or alter the bend of a path to lead the eye into the picture.

There are some basic errors which should be avoided if possible. In general it is not a good idea to divide a landscape horizontally into two equal halves – the land and the sky – as the result will usually be monotonous. A line, such as a path or fence, should not lead directly out of the picture unless balanced by another line which leads the eye back into it. A still life or portrait should not be divided in half vertically, while a flower painting is unlikely to be pleasing to the eye if the flower arrangement is placed too far down in the picture area, too far to one side, or very small in the middle, with a large expanse of featureless background.

In the case of interiors, portraits, still lifes, and flowers, backgrounds can be used as a device to balance the main elements of the composition. Use part of a piece of furniture behind a seated figure, for example, or

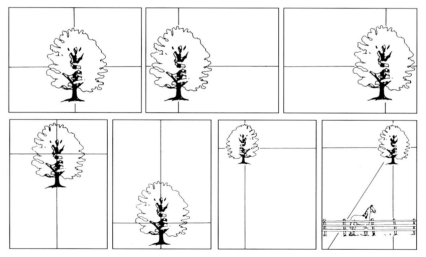

ABOVE: *As the tree is moved to different positions on the picture plane, the composition of the picture is radically changed. Although it is an identical drawing in each case, the composition of each example is quite different, thus illustrating the fact that although the subject matter can be important in making an interesting drawing, it is not necessarily the most important. It is more important that the position of the subject matter within the four sides of the picture plane will make an interesting composition.*

ABOVE: *The natural inclination when painting subjects like trees is to try and get everything in, but in this painting the artist has allowed the foreground trees to "bust" out of the frame, giving a stronger and more exciting effect.*

a subtly patterned wallpaper that echoes or contrasts with the main shapes and colors in the figure. In landscape painting the sky is a vital part of the composition, and should always be given as much care and thought as the rest of the painting.

Even if you are working quickly, it is often helpful to make some drawings, known as thumbnail sketches (though they need not be small) before you start on the painting. These may consist of just a few roughly drawn lines to establish how the main shapes can be placed, or they may help you to work out the tonal pattern of the composition.

Every painter, working in whatever medium, needs to understand the basic rules of the craft, even if sometimes only to break them. The underlying principles of such things as composition, perspective, and drawing itself, apply to all kinds of painting. The novice, who needs to plan his paintings especially carefully, should have a firm grasp of them from the beginning.

CHECKING SHAPES

To draw shapes accurately, it is essential to compare one with another throughout the drawing process. It also helps to use some system of measurement.

It is not easy to make a good outline drawing, or to get shapes in correct proportion with one another. But there are methods that can improve your observational skills.

Suppose you are making a preliminary drawing that includes a tree, and you want to be sure the outline is right before painting. Hold a pencil horizontally at arm's length (see page 86), slide your thumb along it until you have the overall width of the tree, then turn the pencil to a vertical position and see how many times the width goes into the height. The same method can be used for objects in a still life, where you can check not only the height-to-width ratio of each object, but also their different sizes. This is especially helpful when objects are at varying distances from you, since perspective effects can make it easy to misunderstand size and scale.

DRAWING SIGHT SIZE

Some artists always make their drawing or painting the same size as what they see – which does not mean the same as drawing life-size. Try the idea of sight size by placing an object on a table and holding up a piece of paper in front of you at the distance from which you would normally draw. Then close one eye and make two marks, one for each side of the object. It is a little like drawing through a sheet of glass; objects will be the size they register on your retina.

Drawing sight size is easier than attempting to scale things up or down, which often causes shape and angles to go awry. It even allows you to make precise measurements with a ruler held at the level of your work surface. But it can be restrictive, since it sometimes means you must work on a more limited scale than you would like. If you are painting a figure, for example, and cannot go in close, a sight-size drawing will be too small to allow you to give free rein to expressive line, color, or brushwork.

VISUAL REFERENCES

Whether you work sight size or not, slanting shapes and diagonal lines are always hard to assess correctly unless you have some verticals and horizontals to compare them against. When you draw a table from the front, both sides will be diagonals sloping inward. You can determine the angle of these lines more easily if you look at the legs, which provide a vertical reference. Drawing the table top alone is more difficult, which is why people often get this shape wrong in still lifes.

CHECKING AGAINST STRAIGHT LINES

It is difficult to draw anything in isolation because you have nothing to compare it with. You can judge the curve of a chair arm or the angle of an arm or leg in a figure drawing better if there is a straight line behind or next to it.

Vertical and horizontal references are particularly useful in figure drawing, because they help you to understand the lean of the body, the slope of the shoulders, or the angle of an arm or leg. Often you can find background features that provide these, such as a door or window frame.

1 The vertical lines of the wall are sketched in immediately, as they help the artist to assess the angle of the arm. The door behind the figure establishes his size and position in space.

2 With the outline of the radiator draw in, the artist looks at the negative shape between it and the leg, and sees that an adjustment is needed.

3 As a further check, a ruler is held up against the figure and then transferred to the drawing. This shows the artist the exact position of the head in relation to the legs and feet.

SHADOW AND LIGHT IN PAINTING

All the images we see are composed of reflected light – without light we would see nothing. Light can be a very important element of painting. We need light to reveal form, and therefore the direction of light is important. If light falls on a figure from one side of the painting it catches only certain parts of the figures. All solid forms are actually composed of planes, and we understand form because of the way light falls on it. Even a curved surface can be thought of as an infinite number of tiny planes. A change of plane occurs when one plane meets another, and the tone is likely to change at this point because of the different angle of incidence of the light. The change of plane is important in painting because it helps us to explain and represent three-dimensional objects.

The way in which the change of plane occurs depends on the nature of the material. Hard crystalline substances have sharp angular changes, but a soft fabric will have a soft, wavy change of plane. Light, therefore, reveals the form, and the light may itself become the subject of the painting. The patterns cast by falling light dissolve forms, which become a foil for the play of light so that the forms allow us to see the light.

Shadows are useful too; they help to describe spaces and give further clues to the shapes occupied by the forms within the painting. Shadows are obviously dependent on the way the subject is lit. For example, a landscape painted on an afternoon in late winter will have long shadows cast by the weak winter sun that hangs low in the sky. A landscape painted on a summer's day, on the other hand, will be bright and almost shadowless. This will make for a higher-keyed, brighter painting and greater range of colors, whereas the winter scene will have more contrast. Indoors, the light may be natural sunlight falling through a window. The shadows cast by window frames can be incorporated into the painting, and the bright pools of light used to create focal points and draw attention to important features. The subjects of a still life or figure painting can be positioned so that you exploit these light effects. You will have to work quickly, because light changes during the days as the sun climbs through the sky.

PEGGY MATHIAS by Lucy Willis

The painting on page 93 shows the sitter's face strongly lit by the light from a north-facing window.

TONAL VALUES

THE SUNSET HOUR, WEYMOUTH by Arthur Maderson

Tonal key is a term used generally to describe the range of tones within a picture. It tells us about its overall lightness or darkness. It is useful to think in terms of tonal key when first starting to plan your painting, because this will help to determine its mood and emotional impact. By confining his range of tones to the lighter end of the scale, Maderson has conveyed the impression of sparkling light in the picture above. The painting is suffused with that all-pervading brilliance that is characteristic of the successful use of high-key colors.

UNDERSTANDING TONAL VALUES

Painting and drawing are an extension of the art of seeing; by viewing a familiar object in an unexpected way we often gain new insights not only into the physical world around us but also into ourselves and our own individuality. This intensity of experience inevitably comes through in our paintings and drawings, which take on a greater power and beauty.

The word "value" simply refers to how light or dark an area is, whatever its color. Some colors reflect more light than others, which is why we perceive them as being paler in value. For example, navy blue and sky blue are both the same basic color, but navy blue is dark in value, while sky blue is light in value.

In addition, the value of a color is changed by the way the light falls on it, so that one color can show a variety of values. Imagine a man in a navy-blue sweater standing in front of a window so that he is at right-angles to you. His sweater is all made of the same color wool, but you'll notice how its value appears darker at the back than at the front, where the light from the window is striking it.

The idea of tonal values is easy to understand if we look at it in terms of black and white. Every color (every pure, unmixed color, that is) has a tonal "value," ranging from white to black and with infinite shades of gray in between. You can test this by looking at a black and white photograph of a painting, or by adjusting the knob of your color television set

until the picture goes black and white. In black and white, a yellow object looks almost white in value; red and green objects are similar in value, appearing as a middle gray; brown and purple appear dark gray, and so on.

Now we have defined what values are. But why are they so important in painting? Quite simply, the value framework of a picture – the contrast of light and dark areas – can be compared to the skeleton of the human body, or the foundations of a building. Without this solid framework, the whole thing would collapse. In any painting, we have to be aware of the weight of each of the colors we use and how they balance each other, otherwise the picture won't hang together well, nor will it convey a realistic sense of form.

PUTTING IT ALL TOGETHER

Rendering an object or form realistically requires careful observation and an understanding of how tonal values are affected by light. When you are faced with a complex subject such as the human figure, it is easy to become confused by the profusion of lights, halftones, and shadows, so that you lose sight of the main value shapes that describe, for example, the rounded form of the head.

The best way to avoid this sort of confusion is to sit down and make a series of pencil sketches that examine the value pattern of your subject – in other words, the main shapes of light and shade that most clearly describe what is going on. Forget for the minute that you are painting a head, a flower, or a tree, and think purely in terms of patterns of light, medium, and dark values. Try to adopt this analytical approach from the start, for once you understand the logic of how the light is falling on your subject, it will be much easier to express it in your painting.

Every subject has a "local" value that describes how light or dark its actual color is. For example, a red apple is darker than a yellow grapefruit, because red absorbs more light than yellow does. But local values are modified by the effects of light and shade, and it is these modifications that describe the form of an object. So in bright sunlight, the highlight on the red apple might be almost as light in value as the yellow grapefruit is, and similarly, the shaded part of the grapefruit may be almost as dark in value as the red apple.

Thus, the full value range of anything you look at is a combination of local value and the pattern of light and shade falling on the subject. Each has influence on the other – as demonstrated in the figure drawings on page 97. In the first drawing, the artist has blocked in the local values of the model; the local value of the hair is dark, as is the value of the sweater she is wearing. Her face and hands are light, and her skirt is middle in value. The model is lit by a strong overhead light, however, and this creates a definite pattern of light and dark. Now the artist makes a separate drawing, to help him understand the pattern of light and shade falling on the figure. Local values are ignored for the moment.

In the final drawing, we see how the local values and the light and shadow pattern are combined. Remember that the local values will have an influence on the values created by light and shade. Notice, for example, that although the same light is striking both the skin and the hair, the highlights on the skin are lighter than those on the hair, because the local value of the hair

is darker. Similarly, the shadow side of the hair is darker than the shadow side of the face.

It is this interplay between local values and light and shadow that makes a painting visually exciting. The underlying local values lend a harmony and cohesiveness to the image, while the pattern of light and shade playing on the surface creates intriguing light/dark rhythms for the eye to explore and enjoy. Remember that a strong, direct light source will create interesting shadows – and therefore interesting value patterns. With flat, indirect light such as you would find on a hazy day or under fluorescent lights, there are few descriptive shadows and the image is made up of local values only.

Local values . . .

. . . plus light and shade . . .

. . . combine to create form.

THE LANGUAGE OF COLOR

When considering the values and colors in a painting it is useful to know something about their characteristics and the way they react together. Every color has four basic properties: hue, value, chroma, and temperature.

Hue is simply the name given to a color in its purest and simplest form, such as red, green, blue, etc., regardless of variations caused by the way the light falls.

Value refers to the lightness or darkness of a color. For example, light and dark red are of the same hue but different in value. Value contrasts have

great visual impact, but they need to be controlled in order to preserve the unity of the composition.

Chroma refers to the relative intensity or weakness of a color. Colors used straight from the tube are at their most intense; mixing them with other hues reduces their brilliance. For example, cadmium orange is an intense hue, but when mixed with any other color it loses some of that intensity and becomes more neutralized. Pure, intense colors appear even more intense when placed within areas of neutral hue –

CLOSED MONDAYS by Joan Heston

Yellows, blues, pinks, and mauves are subtly woven throughout the composition, activating the entire surface of the painting. The colors are similar in value and intensity, creating a gentle harmony that is appropriate to the subject.

they are emphasized by contrast. Too many intense colors in a painting can have a tiring effect on the eye; in a painting of brightly colored flowers, for example, it is advisable to include some restful neutral passages to provide welcome breathing spaces.

Temperature Colors are referred to as being "warm" or "cool." Reds, oranges and yellows are generally classed as warm, whereas blues, greens, and violets are classed as cool. However, within these divisions

there are varying degrees of warmth and coolness: ultramarine, a blue that contains some red, is warmer than Prussian blue, which veers more toward green. Cadmium red is warmer than alizarin crimson, which has a hint of blue in it. Because warm colors appear to come forward and cool colors to recede, the use of warm hues in the foreground and cool ones in the background creates the effect of depth and atmosphere in landscapes.

COLOR AND VALUE CHARTS

It is important to be able to judge the tone values of your pigments when using them in color mixes. To help you judge value relationships accurately, try making color and value charts like those shown.

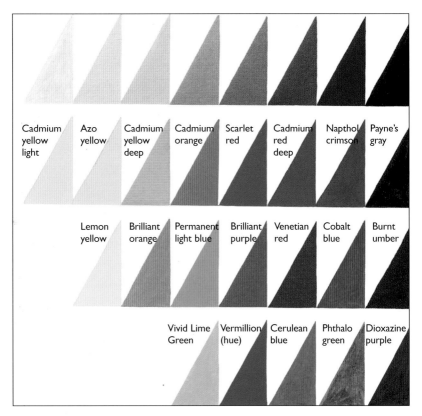

Cadmium yellow light | Azo yellow | Cadmium yellow deep | Cadmium orange | Scarlet red | Cadmium red deep | Napthol crimson | Payne's gray

Lemon yellow | Brilliant orange | Permanent light blue | Brilliant purple | Venetian red | Cobalt blue | Burnt umber

Vivid Lime Green | Vermillion (hue) | Cerulean blue | Phthalo green | Dioxazine purple

Chart A Draw a grid with nine vertical columns, each about 1 in. (2.5 cm) wide. Divide these horizontally into four sections (to create 36 squares or rectangles (you can make more if you wish). Along the top section, make a nine-tone bar, starting with white on the left, going through shades of gray to black on the right in an even gradation of values. Select ten or more colors from your palette, including intense reds, yellows, and blues. Using pure,

unmixed color, fill in the squares on the chart, trying to match each color to its relevant position on the black and white scale. Burnt umber, for instance, is very dark, so it is placed opposite black on the scale.

To test the accuracy of your placings, look at the chart in a dim light, or take a black and white photograph of it. If you have been successful, the chart should appear as four identical, evenly gradated bands of grays.

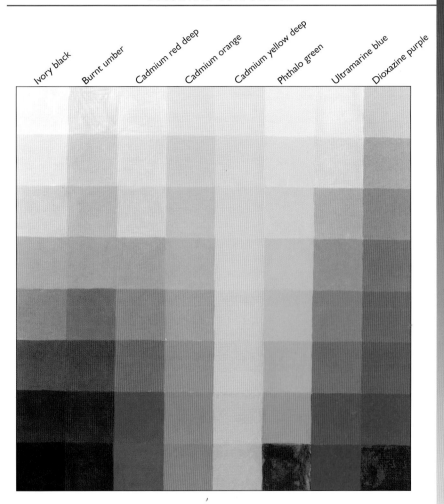

Ivory black Burnt umber Cadmium red deep Cadmium orange Cadmium yellow deep Phthalo green Ultramarine blue Dioxazine purple

Chart B Try a similar exercise, this time aiming to create an even gradation from light to dark within one color. Try it with several colors that are totally different, as in the chart above. This exercise is more difficult than the previous one. You can add white, or more diluent, to lighten the value of a color, but adding black to darken the value can alter the character of the color dramatically. Yellow, for instance, changes to green or brown when black is added.

HOW VALUES AFFECT EACH OTHER

The colors and values in your painting should never be regarded in isolation, but in terms of how they relate to those around them. All colors and values are influenced by neighboring ones, therefore each touch of color you add to a painting alters the relationship of colors already there. For instance, a bright color appears richer when placed next to a neutral or muted color, which reinforces it by contrast. Similarly, a dark value appears even darker when juxtaposed with a light one. Such visual dynamics add greater interest and expressiveness to a painting.

Beginners often tend to work on one small area of the picture until it is "finished," and then move on to the next area. Not only is this a laborious way of working, it also leads to a confused and "jumpy" painting because there is no harmonizing influence to hold everything together.

Try to work on all areas of the picture at once. Work from landscape to sky and back again, or from figure to ground and back again. Keep your eyes moving around the picture, constantly assessing and comparing one color against another. Aim to balance warm colors with cool, intense colors with muted ones, and light values with dark. In this way, your painting will grow and develop in an organic way, emerging finally as a complete unit, a homogeneous mass

Depicting the effect of light on reflective surfaces can be confusing. In this still life the artist has tried to give the impression of a shiny metal vase by piling on a lot of thick white paint for the highlights. The result is weak, like an over-developed negative, because the values in the rest of the image are also light; there is no tonal variation to interest the eye.

of color and value. Painting is a continuous process of balancing, judging, altering, and refining – which is what makes it so absorbing. The examples that follow demonstrate some of the points to watch out for when assessing the relative values and colors in your paintings.

The old axiom that light is produced by sacrifice is demonstrated in this version (right). Notice how the highlights on the vase and the apple appear to glow when surrounded by a large mass of dark values. The values available to us in paint are no match for the range of values found in nature, so a compromise must be made; to make an area of light value suggest brilliance, place it in opposition to strong, contrasting darks. Look at any portrait by Rembrandt and you will see this principle in action.

When modeling form through contrasts of light and shade, remember that strong value contrasts and strong color contrasts do not always work together. In this watercolor sketch below, the artist has used both and the result is garish and overdone.

This study of a pear (right) looks good enough to eat! Here the artist has used minimal color contrasts, relying on value contrasts to express the rounded form of the fruit. Notice the movement around the form from warm light to cool shadow.

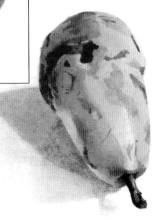

THE ILLUSION OF DEPTH

LANDSCAPE, LATE
AFTERNOON by
Charles Harrington

Perhaps the greatest challenge in landscape painting is that of creating the illusion of space and depth on a flat piece of paper or canvas. The sight of fields, hills, and trees stretching away into the hazy distance is a marvelous one, but how can we capture it convincingly in paint?

Simple tricks of linear perspective can work to a certain extent; overlapping one shape in front of another, for example, gives an instant three-dimensional effect, as does the presence of a foreground detail that recedes into the picture, such as a road or fence. But by far the most effective means of improving the quality of depth and distance in a painting is through the use of "aerial perspective." This term, invented by Leonardo da Vinci (1452–1519) describes the phenomenon found in nature whereby dark forms become darker, with the contrasts between values becoming progressively smaller toward the horizon.

This chapter explains how to use value and color to reproduce the effects of aerial perspective and so bring your landscapes to life. In addition, you'll find advice on how to choose the best viewpoint so as to emphasize the feeling of depth and recession. Finally, you'll discover ways to capture the subtle nuances of value and color that lend a feeling of air and atmosphere to portraits, still lifes, and indoor scenes.

AERIAL PERSPECTIVE

The term "aerial perspective" describes an optical illusion caused by the presence of water vapor and tiny particles of dust in the atmosphere, which act almost like a series of invisible veils strung across the landscape. The farther into the distance we can see, the more "veils" we have to look through, which is why colors and forms appear more hazy and indistinct the closer they are to the horizon.

The effects of aerial perspective are most apparent when there are well-defined planes within the subject, such as a mountain range or a series of cliffs jutting out along a shoreline. They can also be seen clearly when dusk approaches, reducing the forms of the land to almost silhouetted shapes that become lighter in value towards the horizon. This makes it easier to see the changes that occur between the foreground, middle distance, and far distance. Let's say, for example, that you're standing on a hill, surveying an undulating landscape of tree-covered fields and hills. As your eye travels from the foreground to the horizon,

SEA MIST by Clemente Gerez

Here we see the classic effects of aerial perspective. Values and colors fade gradually toward the horizon, and forms become less definite. The diagram (above) shows clearly a receding arrangement of overlapping values, which creates a feeling of depth.

these are the changes you will notice:
Values become altered – Those objects that are closest to you are relatively unaffected by atmospheric haze, so you see their values at full strength. In the middle distance, however, some of the strength of the values is lost, due to the intervening atmosphere, and they appear lighter.

Way back on the horizon, they are weakest of all, seeming to melt into the pale value of the sky. You will also notice, however, that white objects in the distance become darker, not lighter, in value because they are grayed by the atmosphere.
Colors become cooler – Atmospheric haze has the same effect

on color as it has on value. In the foreground, colors appear bright and warm because they are seen at their fullest intensity. In the middle distance, they lose some of their intensity, become cooler and take on a blue cast. Compare a foreground tree, for instance, with a tree 500 yards away, and notice how the color of the foliage changes from a warm yellow-green to a cooler blue-green. Farther back still, a tree may not look green at all, but a subdued blue-gray.

Detail and contrast are diminished – Tonal contrasts – say between a light-colored building and the dark shadow it casts – are sharpest and clearest in the foreground. In the middle distance the intervening haze narrows the range of values and causes contrasts to be less marked, while on the horizon there is often no contrast at all – everything is blurred into one pale value. Similarly, texture and detail become less and less defined the farther you get from the foreground.

So, in order to create the illusion of infinite space and depth in our paintings, all we have to do is to reproduce the effects described previously. Strong values and warm colors appear to come forward, whereas weak values and cool colors appear to recede into the distance – and it is the contrast between these values and colors that gives the illusion of distance.

It seems simple, but inexperienced painters often ignore what they see in front of them and put too much color, detail and clarity into their backgrounds. This is because they have fallen into the familiar trap of painting what they know, instead of what they see: they "know" a tree is supposed to be green, so they paint it green, even though it is miles away on the horizon and actually appears blue. The result is always the same – a flat, unconvincing painting with none of the subtle atmospheric qualities that attracted the artist to the subject in the first place.

WINTER SUNSHINE, LLWYNHIR by Diana Armfield

This landscape conveys a strong impression of space and atmosphere. Notice how the hot colors of the setting sun don't jump forward, but are kept in their place by the stronger value of the large cloud.

COLORS IN AERIAL PERSPECTIVE

Warm and cool colors are useful to painters in many ways. When they are situated in the same plane and at the same distance from the eye the warm colors advance and the cool colors recede. This aspect of color can be used to create a sense of space in a painting. The artist cools the colors in the distance and warms those in the foreground. This can be seen in the work of many landscape painters of the past, who traditionally used blue to describe distant objects. This method of aerial perspective combining warm and cool colors and contrasts of color, tone, and line to create a sense of space is known as aerial perspective. All colors in our world are perceived through the atmosphere. Dust and droplets of moisture cause scattering of light as it passes through the atmosphere, affecting the way we see the colors, which appear to change according to the distance from our eyes. Objects in the distance appear less distinct and take on a bluish tinge, while in the far distance only the broad shapes of objects can be observed, and are perceived as pure blue. The contrasts in tone are greater in the foreground and smaller in the distance, a quality exploited by aerial perspective.

COTTESLOE BEACH, PERTH by Diana Armfield

In this almost abstract composition, an inspired choice of viewpoint evokes the vastness of the ocean. The high horizon line lends impact to the sweep of the water, which cuts diagonally, like an arrow through the composition. This presents an interesting reversal of the normal effects of aerial perspective, in that tones become darker toward the horizon, not lighter.

CHOOSING THE BEST VIEWPOINT

Once you have grasped the principles of aerial perspective, the qualities of depth and atmosphere in your paintings will increase tremendously. However, it is equally important to consider the actual composition of your picture, since this can either enhance the feeling of recession or destroy it.

As we have already seen, the way to achieve depth is to divide your picture into distinct areas in terms of distance – the foreground, middle ground and background – and to keep these areas distinct in value. In this respect, your choice of viewpoint becomes a vital consideration; it can make all the difference between a flat, uninspired picture and an exciting effective one.

Let's look first of all at the center of interest, or focal point – the part of the picture to which the viewer's eye is drawn. This does not necessarily have to be in the forefront of the picture just because it is the center of interest; indeed by placing it in the distance or middle distance, you will

AT THE BEACH by Tom Coates

Here the artist has positioned himself so that the angles of the beach and the background hills form strong directionals that converge in the far distance.

encourage the viewer to "step into" the picture and explore the composition, thereby increasing the impression of distance and depth.

The foreground needs careful thought, too. It should be the strongest of the three planes in the picture, but not so strong that it sets up a barrier between the viewer and the rest of the composition. For this reason, artists such as Camille Corot (1796–1875) included nothing in the foreground of their pictures that was nearer than 200 or 300 yards away from their easels. A slight sketchiness in the immediate foreground is often desirable, especially where the values of the landscape are delicate, as in a misty scene.

On the other hand, a prominent object in the foreground can act as a valuable counterpoint to a more distant center of interest. For example, the overhanging branches of a foreground tree can be used to create a frame within the borders of a picture, through which the viewer looks out across the landscape beyond.

AVIGNON FROM THE WEST (1836) by Jean-Baptiste-Camille Corot

This is one of the many small landscapes painted outdoors by Corot during his summer travels. He kept it in his own collection all his life. He may well have considered it as a study for a larger work to be completed in the winter months, but the compositon is so satisfactory that it is hard to imagine how a different scale might improve it. There is a close relationship between the way in which the artist makes his observations and the scale whereby he translates them into paint.

CONVEYING ATMOSPHERE BY USING SUBDUED VALUES

SASKIA, MORNING by Ken Howard

This scene has a still, timeless quality reminiscent of the paintings of the Dutch Masters. By using subdued values and colors, and "lost and found" edges, the artist conveys the atmosphere of a room enveloped in the soft shadows of late afternoon.

The atmosphere present in an indoor scene is much less apparent than in a landscape, but nevertheless we have to be able to capture it if our paintings are to have a sense of three-dimensional reality.

Look up from this page for a few minutes and survey the room around you. Can you spot the differences in value between, say, a dark object placed close to you and a dark object on the other side of the room? Observe closely a group of objects near the window. Because they're directly in the path of the light, the forms are well defined and the values are strongly contrasted. Now look over at the darkest corner of the

room: do you see how the values there appear much more muted and details and edges are much softer and less defined?

Having trained your eye to notice the effects of atmosphere on objects, the next stage is to record your observations on paper or canvas. Unfortunately, this is where many amateur painters — and some professionals, too — come unstuck. In their obsession with making things look "real," they portray everything with the same degree of clarity, and build up the painting rather like a jigsaw so that each object is trapped within a rigid outline and thus totally divorced from the atmosphere surrounding it.

In order to create the illusion of depth and atmosphere in a painting, you have to mimic the way the eye actually perceives things. If you hold this book up in front of you and look hard at it, everything in the background appears comparatively out of focus. If you then switch your gaze to the background, the book will appear blurred. The point is that since the human eye does not see everything with equal clarity, there is no reason to paint everything with equal clarity. The way to achieve

realism is by emphasizing what is close (by using clear colors and precise outlines) and playing down what is farther away (by softening the contours and modifying the values and colors). This applies even if you are painting a single object, such as a vase of flowers or a portrait head: here, too, the illusion of round, three-dimensional form is achieved by blurring the outlines farthest away and keeping the sharp-focus effects for the immediate foreground.

Don't forget that a good painting or drawing often has a slightly ethereal quality to it. By contrasting hard edges with soft ones, bright colors with muted ones, and sharp detail with sketchiness, you will contribute greatly to the poetry of the painting.

STILL LIFE: REDCURRANTS AND BLACKCURRANT JAM by Pamela Kay

Observe the subtle contrasts that give three-dimensional depth to this still life. The foreground objects, for instance, are clearly stated, whereas the basket of eggs at the back of the group is less defined. The warm red berries bring the foreground closer, while the cool blues in the background are recessive.

TOP: THE GIFT OF SPRING by Urania Christy

When a subject contains bright color masses like this, the local colors partially define the different elements. But color relationships are modified by surface texture, depth, distance, and atmospheric effects.

LEFT: DOG ROSES by Diana Armfield

Even in a study of a single object you need to create an impression of air and space around your subject. Here the outer edges of the leaves and flowers are not hard but softly blended into the background color, particularly at the back of the arrangement. The background itself is painted with broken colors that convey light and movement.

CREATING MOOD

So far we've looked at ways of using tonal values to describe the physical aspects of what we see – in rendering the character and solidity of objects and the nearness and farness of things, for example. But the emotional content of a picture is every bit as important, if not more so. Mood, atmosphere, a certain intangible quality conveyed by the way light falls on a subject – these combine to create "the spell that charges the commonplace with beauty," to quote from the great British photographer Bill Brandt.

Here, once again, tonal values play a major role in creating the mood you want to convey in your pictures. There is a strong connection between the value range in a painting and the mood it conveys; a preponderance of dark values gives a somber or mysterious atmosphere, whereas light values create a lively or cheerful impression.

The way light and dark values are arranged and distributed can also have an influence on the emotional impact of a painting. For example, dark values in the lower half of the painting convey a feeling of strength and stability; but if the dark values occupy the upper half of the composition, as in a storm scene, the mood alters radically, becoming somber and threatening.

SHEEP IN THE SNOW by Diana Armfield

This painting conveys the stark mood of a bitterly cold winter's day. Notice how dark in value the snow is, particularly in the foreground where the shadows are a cool blue.

INTENSIFYING MOOD WITH SHADOWS

As a child I used to love lying in front of the living room fire on winter evenings and watch as the light from the flickering flames sent huge, liquid shadows leaping and dancing around the walls of the room. The shadows of chairs, teacups, and potted plants, distorted and elongated, turned into fairies and witches and monsters in my still-fertile imagination.

Filmmakers have always known how to use the dramatic potential of shadows to intensify the emotional effect of a scene. We've all gripped our seats while watching a thriller in which someone is being followed down a dimly lit street; we don't get to see the mysterious follower – only his shadow cast on the pavement – and this makes our imagination begin to work overtime. Somehow, being able to see only the shadow heightens the tension and has a far more

menacing effect than if the identity of the man were revealed.

The same power of suggestion can be used to great effect in a painting, turning an ordinary image into one that's arresting, mysterious and evocative. Rembrandt achieved powerful dramatic moods through his use of deep, luminous shadows that enveloped most of the subject, just leaving a telling highlight here and there. Salvador Dali (b. 1904) and Giorgio de'Chirico (1888–1978) used very long or distorted shadows to accentuate the timeless, dreamlike atmosphere in their Surrealist paintings. The American painter Edward Hopper (1882–1967) painted people isolated within stark interiors or on deserted streets, and once again cast shadows are used to heighten the sense of loneliness and alienation.

But shadows are not always dramatic or threatening; they can also introduce beauty and poetry to a painting. Most landscape painters prefer to work in the early morning or late afternoon, when the sun is at a low angle to the earth and trees and buildings cast long, descriptive shadows. My own favorite painting

time is late afternoon on a sunny day in autumn, when everything is bathed in a soft, golden light and the lengthening shadows lend a magical air of calm and stillness to the scene.

When a cast shadow travels across another object that lies in its path, that object becomes much more interesting to look at. In Jane Corsellis's painting, see how the shadows cast by the window frame travel across the contours of the bedding and the figure in a flowing, liquid pattern that transforms this everyday scene into a compelling picture. In addition to describing three-dimensional form, the graphic lines of the shadows offer an interesting paradox. Unconsciously we shift back and forth between seeing the shadows as a descriptive element and as a purely abstract pattern. In this way our imagination is fueled and we play an active part in the work.

Carry a sketchbook with you whenever you can and make visual notes of any interesting shadow patterns you come across, such as those cast by a tree, or a wrought-iron gate, or the dappled shadows of trees and plants on a garden path. Indoors you can experiment by moving a lamp around the room, shining it on objects from different heights and angles to see what kind of shadows it creates (adjustable desk lamps are great for this).

FAR LEFT: SARA ASLEEP by Jane Corsellis

This painting is positively alive with light. The highlights and shadows cast by the window travel over the contours of the sleeping figure and the bedding in a flowing, liquid pattern. The mood is one of warmth, relaxation, and intimacy.

CHOOSING COLORS

Color is an extremely complex subject, and its study falls within several disciplines: physics, chemistry, physiology, and psychology. Physicists study the electromagnetic vibrations and particles involved in the phenomenon of light; chemists look at the properties of dyes and pigments; physiologists are interested in the way the eye and the brain allow us to experience color, and psychologists look at our awareness of color and the way in which this affects us. The artist must be aware of all these considerations, but each discipline defines color in a different way, which can cause a great deal of confusion. Here, we restrict ourselves to some of those aspects of color theory that will be of immediate use to you as an artist.

It is more than 300 years since Sir Isaac Newton found the color in light and discovered the light spectrum in the course of a historical experiment. He directed a beam of sunlight into a glass prism, and because glass is denser than air the light rays were bent, or "refracted," as they passed through the prism. The light that emerged from the prism was separated into the band of colors we now know as the solar spectrum. The colors of the refracted spectrum range in a continuous band from red through orange, yellow, green, blue, and indigo to violet. If these colors are collected again by means of a converging lens they will combine to form white light once more.

The artist, however, is concerned with the color of refracted light rather than that of direct light, an important distinction to bear in mind, because it explains the difference between the color of light and the color of pigments.

The color wheel, color circle, color sphere, and color tree are all devices by which artists have sought to come to terms with color and to explain their theories. Various circles have been suggested containing from six to 24 colors. The color wheel illustrated on page 117 has six colors: red, orange, yellow, green, blue, and violet. Complementary colors are those that are directly opposite each other and therefore most widely separated on the color wheel. Yellow and violet, and red and green, are examples of complementary colors. Each of these pairs of colors combines to make gray. They and their effects are very important in the way we perceive color, and therefore vital to painting.

If you have never used oil paints before, obviously the first and most important thing you have to decide is which tubes of paint to buy, so let's look at a suitable range of "starter" colors. It is best to limit yourself to the really essential ones to begin with – you can always add more. As all colors are mixed with white, you must have a large tube of titanium white, not flake white. Add to this two reds (alizarin crimson and cadmium red); three yellows (cadmium, lemon, and yellow ocher); two blues (ultramarine and Prussian or phthalocyanine blue); one brown (raw umber); one green (viridian), and one black (ivory black). That's eleven colors, which is plenty. Some artists would rule out the black, but it's marvelous in mixtures – never use it on its own.

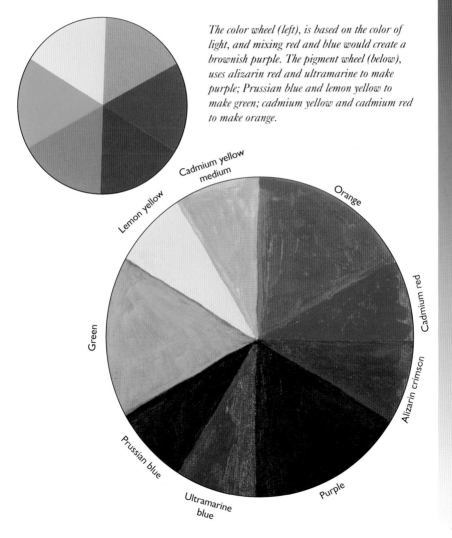

The color wheel (left), is based on the color of light, and mixing red and blue would create a brownish purple. The pigment wheel (below), uses alizarin red and ultramarine to make purple; Prussian blue and lemon yellow to make green; cadmium yellow and cadmium red to make orange.

Cadmium yellow medium

Lemon yellow

Orange

Green

Cadmium red

Prussian blue

Alizarin crimson

Ultramarine blue

Purple

Later on you will certainly want to extend your range, and your choice of extras will depend on your subject matter. On page 167 there are some suggestions for indispensable flower colors, but if you are committed to landscape you are more likely to want more greens and browns. Whatever you choose, until you are sure a color is suited to your needs, buy small tubes rather than full-sized ones. And whatever you do, don't fall for colors with names like "flesh tint" – the only way to make flesh look real is by mixing.

MOUNT ZION by David Graham

Experimenting with color is one of the most exciting aspects of painting. The light, bright, "high-key" colors in this landscape may not be exactly as they were in reality, but they convey a powerful impression of sunshine and heat.

LEFT: *Bright colors can be made to appear even more vivid by contrasting them with neutral or dark ones. In this delightfully simple still life, the artist has boldly devoted some two-thirds of the painting to the almost black background, so that the colors of the fruit sing out like a fire in the night.*

RIGHT: *A painting is unlikely to be successful unless it has an overall unity of color, and this picture derives its atmosphere of peace and serenity from the way the colors have been chosen and controlled. The patches of light yellow sunlight provide the "key," and all the other colors – darker yellows, warm mauves, and red-golds – are orchestrated around them.*

WARM AND COOL COLORS

The color circle can be divided into two groups: the "warm" colors and the "cool" colors. The yellow-greens, yellows, oranges, and reds are generally regarded as warm colors and the greens, blues, and violets are considered to be cool. A reaction to color in terms of warm and cool is obviously subjective and people vary in the extent to which they perceive color temperature – some people are almost unaware of the distinction. But by looking at colors in this way you will find that the warm, fiery ones do convey a very different feeling from their color opposites. When we describe colors as warm or cool, we are not, of course, referring to physical qualities, but to aesthetic qualities of the colors. Some colors fall rather obviously into one or other of the categories, others are more difficult to place.

The inherently hot colors are the cadmiums, cadmium yellows and reds, and their derivatives. These colors are at their most intense and dynamic when used in pure form straight from the tube. Despite these classifications, there are warm blues and cool reds for example, ultramarine and cerulean are warm blues, whereas alizarin and light red are cool reds.

The degree of warmth and coolness of a color depends very much on how you juxtapose them and what you mix with them. Lemon yellow is cool when placed next to warm cadmium yellow, but the same lemon yellow would be perceived as warm if placed beside Prussian blue.

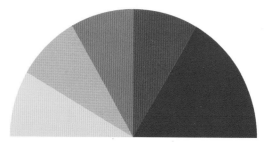

The warm colors are generally defined as the bright yellows, oranges, and reds. These are colors you would naturally associate with heat. Red-purple is variable, but can appear warm.

Greens, blues, and blue-purples are typically regarded as cool colors. A true purple is borderline, since it contains equal influences of red and blue.

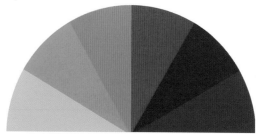

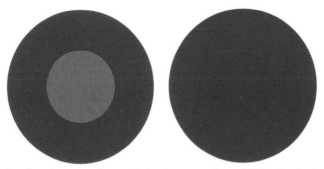

The fiery hue of orange red seems obviously warmer than mid-blue, but the degree of contrast is not easy to identify when it is matched with crimson, a blue-tinged red that can appear warm or cool.

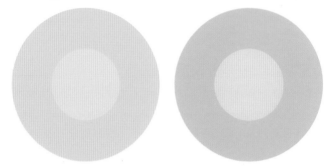

Although yellows are defined as warm, lemon yellow has a greenish tinge that can make it seem cool, whether compared to sunshine yellow or to the cool, but deep-toned green.

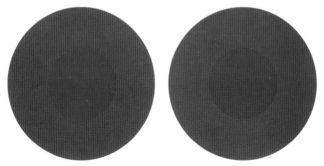

Purples and blues react variably to each other and their relationship is quite complex. Purple, mauve, and ultramarine are all dark-toned, and their density can enhance the warmth of their degrees of red bias.

MIXING COLORS

Learning to mix colors is the first step toward achieving a successful painting. Initially it is certain to involve some trial and error, but there are some general guidelines to bear in mind.

The very first experience with mixing can be with just white and black, before trying out the other colors. It is slightly easier to judge tones and tints of gray than the tones and tints of primaries and secondaries. This exercise is basic to all the color-mixing exercises. It will incorporate

mixing, applying, and experiencing the visual impact of tone, tint, and hue.

Mixtures should be well integrated, on the palette, with a knife, and with enough fluidity to allow the brush to make a good, clean stroke.

For the kind of grid that will suit this exercise best, use six squares, about $1/2$ in. (1.2 cm) in size, which can be conveniently filled with variegated tones of paint from light to dark, and from dark to light.

Method 1

Add black to white, to make a series of grays, from the palest to the darkest tints, in six steps. The gray of medium strength should occur in the center of the scale.

Method 2

Reverse the process by adding white to black.

This exercise can now be repeated with all the colors on your palette, one by one, utilizing Method 1 to make tones, and Method 2 to make tints. There is no need to paint them carefully, if your natural inclination is to paint them freely. The practice should be as enjoyable as possible. The only proviso is that care should be taken in the mixing of the paint, so that each change of tone, in its respective square, is as clear as possible.

The aim of this exercise is to sharpen sensitivity, and give valuable experience not only in mixing color, but to see what the color looks like when mixed.

Any flat, nonabsorbent surface can be used as the palette, but whether it is a conventional kidney-shaped one or simply a piece of glass it must always be large enough to enable you to arrange the tube colors around the edges while allowing plenty of room in the center for mixing.

The tube colors should be arranged in some sort of order so that you can always find the one you are looking for (the dark colors in their pure form look very similar). Some artists arrange colors from light to dark, with white and black as opposite poles. Others prefer to group all the warm colors (reds, yellows, browns, etc.) together at one end and all the cool ones (blues, greens, and acid yellows) at the other. You are more likely to mix warm with warm and cool with cool than to combine both in one mixture.

LIGHT AND DARK MIXTURES

It is usually best to restrict mixtures to no more than three colors, as this reduces the risk of muddying. Care has to be taken when mixing any color with white, as although this lightens the tone, it does so in unpredictable ways, and sometimes also changes the hue. The reds, for example, become pink as soon as white is added. The tinting power of pigments varies considerably. Raw umber becomes very pale when mixed with white, even in small quantities, as does terre verte, a deep green when unmixed. Colors such as these are best used neat, or mixed with other dark colors for shadow areas. Alizarin crimson and Prussian

Treated wooden palettes are traditionally used for oil paints. Many artists lay out their colors in a sequence, such as light to dark, along the edge of the palette and mix into the middle.

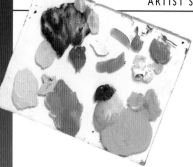

blue, on the other hand, only have to be added to white in small quantities to produce quite vivid colors, so for pale tints, always start with the white and add color little by little.

The addition of black to any color will darken the tone, but in some cases can lead to muddying, so it can be more satisfactory to darken with brown, green, or blue. However, black is a most useful color on the palette, and mixing it with a strong yellow, such as cadmium or Indian yellow, produces a wonderfully rich olive green.

COMPLETE AND PARTIAL MIXING

Colors can be mixed with a palette knife or a bristle brush, the former being more suitable for thick impasto work. Mixing with a brush can wear down the bristles; it is a good idea to keep old brushes specifically for this purpose rather than using painting brushes.

As a general rule, colors should be mixed thoroughly or the brush strokes will be streaky. However, this is an effect that can be exploited deliberately; for example, streaks of pure green appearing in a brown-

green mixture for a tree trunk or wooden building can be more descriptive than flat color. Some artists take this method further by using two or even three separate color mixtures, taking up a little of each on the brush so that they remain separate within the brush stroke.

This partial mixing gives an effect very much like working wet into wet, where the colors blend on the picture surface. There are also other methods of mixing color on the support itself, such as dry brush, glazing and scumbling, all of which can be used to modify a color by adding further layers.

Partial mixing is sometimes an accidental result of not having cleaned brushes thoroughly between one color and the next, but it can be exploited deliberately. Mix up two or more colors separately and then pick up a little of each so that the same brush stroke incorporates more than one color.

Everyone knows that the three primary colors are red, blue, and yellow. However, there are many different versions of the primaries, so those new to the painting will have to find out the different kind of mixtures each will produce. This triangle shows the "warmer" primaries, with the secondary colors made from them in the inner triangles and a mixture of all three secondaries in the center.

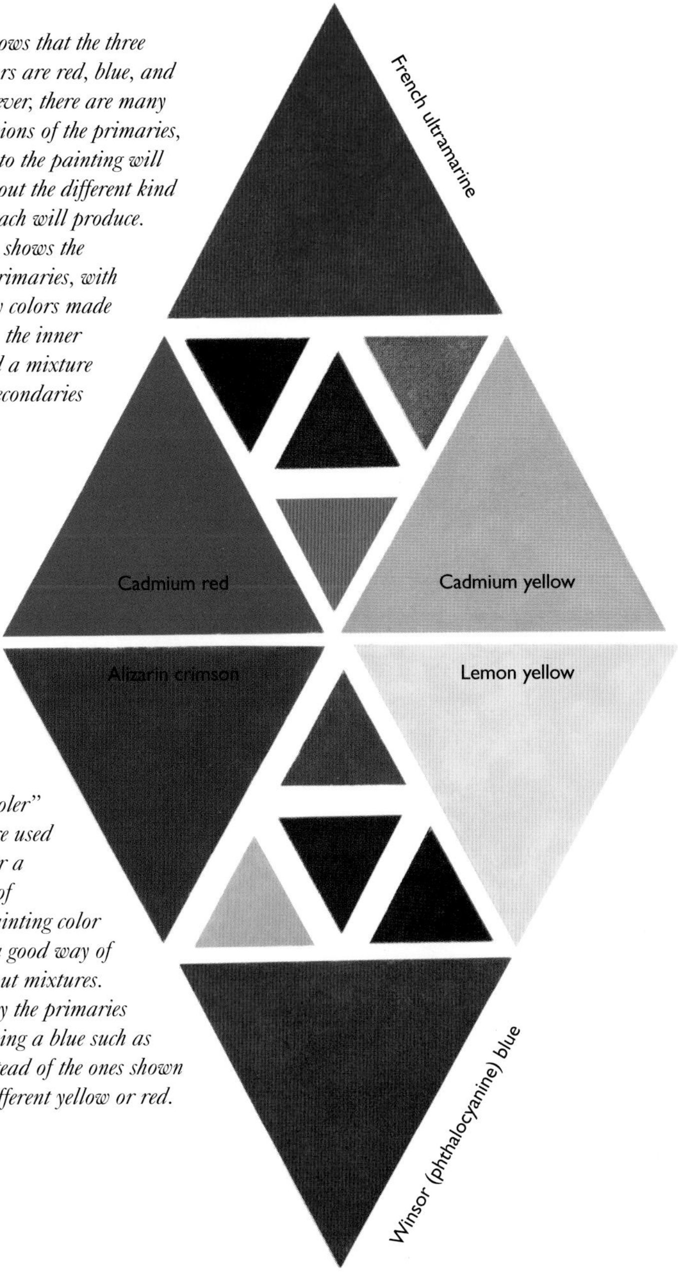

French ultramarine

Cadmium red

Cadmium yellow

Alizarin crimson

Lemon yellow

Here the "cooler" primaries are used as a basis for a different set of mixtures. Painting color triangles is a good way of learning about mixtures. You can vary the primaries further by using a blue such as cerulean instead of the ones shown here, or a different yellow or red.

Winsor (phthalocyanine) blue

LIGHTENING AND DARKENING COLORS

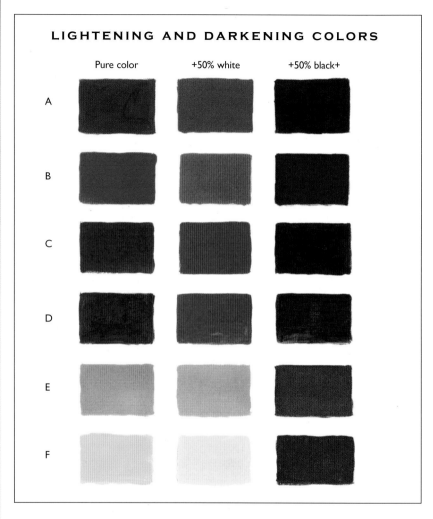

	Pure color	+50% white	+50% black+
A			
B			
C			
D			
E			
F			

KEY TO CHART
Colors
A Alizarin crimson
B Cadmium red
C French ultramarine
D Winsor (phthalocyanine) blue
E Cadmium yellow
F Lemon yellow

This chart shows how some colors behave when they are mixed with first white and then black. As you will see, reds change their character in both cases, so it is often more satisfactory to lighten them with another color such as yellow and darken with blue or another red.

MIXING ON THE CANVAS

Oil paint is a substantial but slow-drying medium, so although you can mix colors accurately and apply bold, opaque strokes, you need to work methodically to avoid mixing and muddying the colors on the canvas. James Horton has used a broken color technique, putting down dabs of color side by side to achieve the variations of hue and tone gradually.

1 The composition is sketched out with a thinned mixture of raw umber and Indian red. The artist begins directly to set up an overall color balance, blocking in the local colors of the objects with small brush strokes. For the mid-toned colors – the blues, greens, and reds – he introduces slight tonal variations to suggest light and shadow.

2 The same process continues until the image area is gradually covered with color. Variations and contrasts are emphasized by using different colors for the mixing base; for example, cerulean blue for the green-blue and ultramarine for the mid-blues and purples.

Similarly, the artist offsets the cool bluish-pink made with alizarin crimson and white with a "hot" tint based on cadmium red.

3 The artist continues building up with small strokes until all the shapes are blocked in with a solid layer of color. He then uses longer and broader strokes to blend the tones within each color area, helping to model the forms. Linear detail suggesting the texture of the wool is over-painted with a fine, pointed sable brush.

4 The pattern on the tablecloth is finely traced, and the cast shadows on the left of the basket are strengthened using a neutral tint mixed from raw umber and titanium white, modified with cadmium orange or with ultra-

marine to deepen the shade. Minor adjustments are made where necessary to enhance the tonal structure.

5 In the final stage (far right), the artist works in loose, vigorous strokes, adding vibrancy to the bright hues and depth to the shadow colors. Subtle color contrasts are brought out more strongly, such as the juxtaposition of blue-green with yellow-green, and blue-purple against violet, in the two balls of wool placed in front of the basket.

THE EFFECTS OF MIXING

The kind of mixed color you will obtain from particular combinations depends basically upon whether the colors are alike or unlike, and what biases or undertones they have that may be introducing an element of yet another color. The following are basic principles that will apply when you mix two colors only:

◆ Mixing two hues from the same color family results in a relatively pure, clean hue that combines their characteristics. A mix of two reds produces another slightly different red, and so on.

◆ Mixing two separate hues from different families in certain cases will produce a clean combination that makes a third color of distinctly individual character – such as yellow and red for orange, yellow, and blue for green.

◆ Mixing two hues that are directly related or share some color quality gives a third, intermediate hue that may tend to one or another of the original components. For example, blue and green form a blue-green or green-blue, with no devaluation because blue is a component of

green. Red and red-violet produce a redder violet or a violet-tinged red.

◆ Mixing two hues that are visually unlike results in a quite different, usually neutralized color. Certain kinds of red and blue make violet, but often a blue-red mixture forms a kind of brown. Blue-and-orange or red-and-green mixes make shades of brown. Yellow and violet mixes make a kind of dark yellow or mauve-gray, depending on proportions in the mix, or a brownish color if the violet is biased to red.

◆ Mixing a hue with white or black lightens or darkens the color, but it may also change it to produce another kind of color. Red and white, for example, produce pink; red and black make brown; yellow and black make green. A tint made by adding white, however, has a color value different from that of a lighter tone of the original hue made by diluting the paint; and the addition of black can deaden the "colorfulness" of the hue's influence in the mixture.

When you start to make mixtures that contain three or more colors, the results more rapidly become muddy and less colorful. This is partly because the different pigment particles are partially "masking" each other, and partly because you are likely to be mixing colors that are unlike, or have dissimilar characteristics. If you mix a tube green with some yellow and

blue, you may obtain a different, perfectly acceptable shade of green. But if the yellow is orangey, you are introducing a touch or red that "opposes" the green and takes down it vibrancy and intensity. Three- and four-color mixes can produce interesting neutrals, however, and if white is one of the components, you obtain the range that we describe by

terms such as beige, buff, and "colored grays." Remember to always rinse and blot your brushes whenever you change colors, and freshen your turpentine frequently.

OPACITY AND STRENGTH OF COLOR

Another important thing to understand when you are mixing colors is that different pigments have different properties, some being more opaque than others. This affects their mixing capabilities, and if used unmixed, their ability to cover an underlying color. Opaque pigments such as oxide of chromium green have strong covering power, while sap green is transparent. Instead of obliterating a color below, it will modify it by adding its own quality. You can see some of these differences in the chart below:

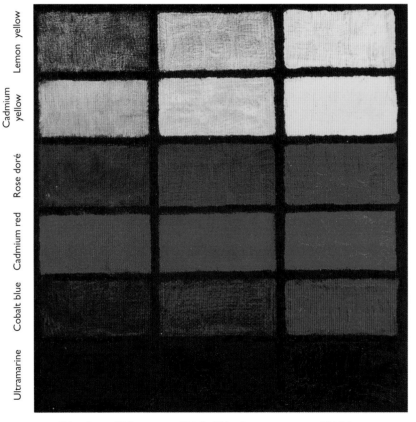

| Painted very thinly | Slightly thicker layer | Thick layer |

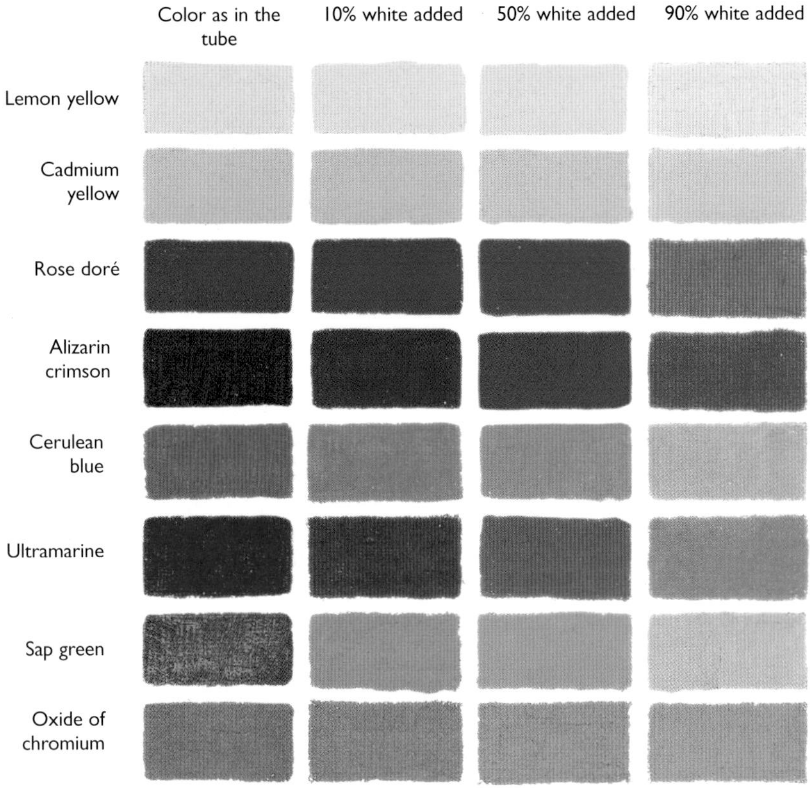

	Color as in the tube	10% white added	50% white added	90% white added
Lemon yellow				
Cadmium yellow				
Rose doré				
Alizarin crimson				
Cerulean blue				
Ultramarine				
Sap green				
Oxide of chromium				

In the context of color mixing, an even more important factor is the strength of the color. Some colors will dominate others in a mixture, and have to be used in smaller amounts. Strength of color is not related to opacity. Alizarin crimson, for example, is very strong but transparent, while cerulean blue is weak but semi-opaque. A transparent color can be made opaque by adding white, but its strength will determine how much it is lightened in the process.

When white is added to a color it often has the effect of cooling it as well as lightening it. As you can see from the chart above, this is particularly noticeable with the reds, which change from warm, vivid colors to quite cool pinks. This is because the warm end of the spectrum of light is partially blocked by the white pigment, leaving a higher proportion of cooler light rays (i.e. more blue).

OPTICAL MIXING

The French painter Georges Seurat and others used to put small dabs or strokes of contrasting colors next to each other on the canvas, so that from a distance they would "mix" in the eye of the viewer. This, called Pointillism, creates a lively impression and modified versions of the technique are still used today. For the best results, the colors must be close in tone (i.e. of a similar lightness or darkness). Here are some examples – you may need to hold the book away from you so that the "optical mixing" can take place.

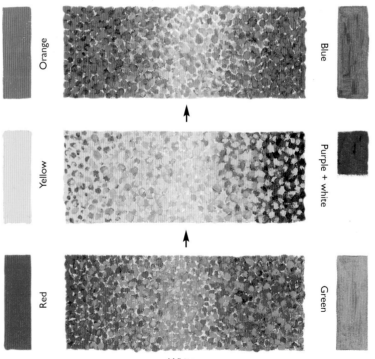

MIXING SKIN TONES

The number of different words we use for describing the color of skin – cream, peaches, gold, coffee, ebony, and so on – points up the fact that skin tones vary widely. In addition, the colors are affected by lighting conditions and surrounding colors, particularly of clothing. It is at least as important to pitch the tones (the lights and darks) correctly as to find

VERY DARK COMPLEXION

Alizarin crimson with raw umber + Prussian blue

MID-BROWN COMPLEXION

Burnt umber, yellow ocher, cadmium orange + white

SHADOWS

Alizarin crimson + Prussian blue

Alizarin crimson + viridian

Payne's gray

SHADOWS

Raw umber

Ultramarine

Raw umber + cadmium red

HIGHLIGHTS

Naples yellow

Cadmium red + white

Cobalt blue + white

HIGHLIGHTS

Cadmium yellow + white

Lemon yellow + white

Cadmium red + white

the "right" colors, and artists often take liberties with colors to achieve effects that, while not strictly realistic, may enhance the appearance of living flesh. But although it is not possible to suggest a suitable palette for all skin, some suggestions can be made. Here we show four suggested basic colors, to which further colors can be added for shadows and highlights.

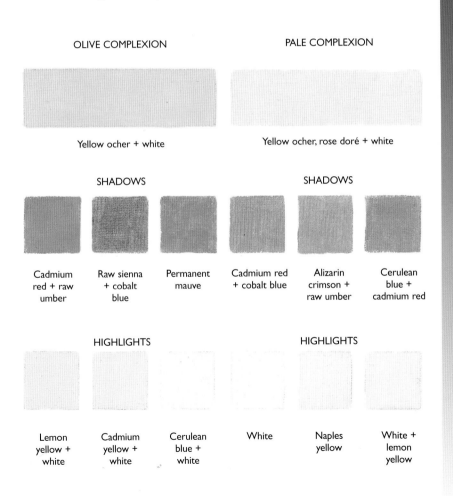

OLIVE COMPLEXION

Yellow ocher + white

PALE COMPLEXION

Yellow ocher, rose doré + white

SHADOWS

Cadmium red + raw umber

Raw sienna + cobalt blue

Permanent mauve

SHADOWS

Cadmium red + cobalt blue

Alizarin crimson + raw umber

Cerulean blue + cadmium red

HIGHLIGHTS

Lemon yellow + white

Cadmium yellow + white

Cerulean blue + white

HIGHLIGHTS

White

Naples yellow

White + lemon yellow

THE ARTISTS:
AND THEIR INFLUENCE

Our century has seen a proliferation of art movements, and artists have felt free to work in whatever way they wished. New media such as acrylic and alkyd have come onto the market and found favor with many painters, but oil paint has lost none of its attraction – rather, its possibilities have been extended beyond anything that could have been imagined by previous masters of the medium. Salvador Dali (*b.*1904), for example, sought a kind of photographic realism, applying oil paints in a way which was obviously derived from the Flemish masters. In his search for minute accuracy he often worked with a jeweler's glass, resting his arm on a mahl stick.

EDGAR DEGAS
1840 • 1926

Edgar Degas was born Hilaire-Germain-Edgar Degas on July 19, 1834, in Paris, France. In 1855 he enrolled at the famous École des Beaux-Arts, or School of Fine Arts, in Paris. To supplement his studies, Degas traveled extensively, including trips to Naples, Florence, and Rome (where he lived for three years), in order to observe and copy the works of such Renaissance masters as Sandro Botticelli, Andrea Mantegna, and Nicolas Poussin. Degas learned a good deal about drawing figures, a skill that he used to complete some impressive family portraits.

Degas' style after the early 1860s was influenced by the budding Impressionist movement, including his friendship with Édouard Manet.

Many of Degas' paintings featured the artist's experiments with unorthodox visual angles and asymmetrical perspectives, somewhat like a photographer's treatment of a subject. Examples of this style are *A Carriage at the Races* (1872), which features a human figure who is almost cut in half by the edge of the canvas, and *Ballet Rehearsal* (1876), a group portrait of ballerinas that appears almost cropped at the edges. From 1873 to 1883, Degas produced many of his most famous works, both paintings and pastels, of his favorite subjects, including the ballet, the racecourse, the music hall, and café society.

Sometime in the 1870s, Degas began to suffer a loss of vision, which limited his ability to work. He began increasingly to work as a sculptor, producing bronze statues of horses and ballet dancers, among other subjects.

Degas was one of the great innovators and promoters of pastels. He experimented widely with different techniques and developed a painting method that involved spraying the pastel surface with warm water or milk. Degas' use of gesture and color are important aspects to study. He was also one of the first artists to use broken color – strokes of pure color that mix optically.

Edgar Degas was also fascinated by the effects of artificial lighting and sometimes transferred the elements of theatricality into a portrait in a domestic interior. The following quotation, taken from *The Notebooks of Edgar Degas*, is an example of the advice he gave to others: "Work a great deal at evening effects, lamp light etc. The intriguing thing is not to show the source of light but the effect of the lighting." Degas realized that by not revealing the source of the light he could take more liberties with its effects.

PORTRAIT OF DIEGO MARTELLI by Edgar Degas

The placement of the figure in the picture plane is an important element in figure work. Note in this painting Degas' skillful balancing of the figure with other objects as well as areas of strong highlights and shadow.

CLAUDE MONET
1834 • 1917

AUTUMN AT ARGENTEUIL by Claude Monet

The French Impressionists were very much influenced by Constable's landscape paintings, and Monet in particular took the preoccupation with the effects of light almost to the point of an obsession. He frequently worked outdoors and would paint several versions of the same scene in different lights in order to achieve the effect which he sought.

Claude Monet was born November 14, 1840, in Paris, France and was a rudimentary figure in the evolution of Impressionism. In 1845 his family moved to Le Havre, and by the time he was 15, Monet had developed a local reputation as a caricaturist. Eugène Boudin, a landscape painter, exerted a profound influence on the young Monet. Boudin introduced him to outdoor painting, an activity that he entered reluctantly but which soon became the basis for his life's work.

Monet was intrigued by the phenomena of natural light, atmosphere, and color captivated his imagination. He committed himself to an increasingly accurate recording of their fascinating variety. A striking example of his early style is *Terrace at Sainte-Adresse* (1867). This painting contains a shimmering array of bright, natural colors, eschewing completely

the somber browns and blacks of the earlier landscape tradition. Monet seldom worked on the same picture for more than two hours at a time in a day. Within two hours, color values can change considerably. The ideal arrangement for a painting of any size is to work for a short period over several days, or weeks if necessary. If this is not possible the size of the picture must be considered accordingly.

Monet's paintings from the 1870s reveal the major principles of Impressionism. *Sunrise*, and *Red Boats at Argenteuil* (1875) are outstanding examples of this style. Working directly from nature, Monet discovered that even the darkest shadows and the gloomiest days contain an infinite variety of colors. To capture the fleeting effects of light and color, however, Monet gradually

BEACH AT TROUVILLE by Claude Monet

This painting has a strong sense of design; the characteristic shape of the umbrellas serves to provide a link from one side of the composition to the other. Monet's sense of visual judgment was so acute, that he was able to place the elements in his compositions intuitively, rather than by relying on mathematical formulas. The placement of the chair roughly relates to the Golden Section, and prevents the composition from becoming too symmetrical.

learned that he had to paint quickly and to employ short brush strokes loaded with individualized colors. This technique resulted in canvases that were charged with activity.

Monet wanted to paint what he saw rather than what he intellectually knew. And he saw not separate leaves, but splashes of constantly changing light and color. Monet definitely belongs to the tradition of Renaissance illusionism: in recording the phenomena of the natural world, he simply based his art on perceptual rather than conceptual knowledge. Over the years as his style matured and as he continued to develop the sensitivity of his vision, the strictly illusionistic aspect of his paintings began to disappear.

JOHN CONSTABLE
1776 • 1837

John Constable was born in East Bergholt, Suffolk on June 11, 1776 and even as a child he showed great interest in art. After completing a year as an apprentice miller in his father's flour mill, he went to London in 1799 to study painting at the Royal Academy schools.

Constable concentrated on the particular sensations received from certain scenes in nature. Comparisons can be made between Constable and the poet Wordsworth. Each loved the familiar and they never turned their backs on the countryside where they grew up. There was an element of sadness, even pessimism, in Constable's later work, and there may well have been an element of nostalgia too, for by the 1820s there was much unemployment and poverty in country life that he would not have been affected by as a child. But it was his interest in the familiar that gave his work its strength. He would work extensively from the same view before attempting the finished canvas. First he made rapid pencil drawings in notebooks, followed by rapid paintings in oil, then more detailed drawings and

VIEW OF WIVENHOE PARK by John Constable

Constable demonstrates here how much can be achieved with the pencil alone. The forms of the landscape are firmly established in space, but also the quality and texture of each part is given due weight. The cornfield in the foreground has its own character defined with the simplest of means, and the delicate treatment of the sky is equally sensitive to light and texture.

larger paintings. One of his many qualities was an ability to hold on to his original conception of the work and develop and refine it by constant study.

John Constable died in 1837 and is buried in Hampstead alongside his beloved Maria. During his lifetime he gained little acclaim in his home country for painting unfashionable landscapes. Yet he is now considered one of the most unique and perhaps the greatest of all British landscape artists.

SALISBURY CATHEDRAL by John Constable

Constable used here a compositional device that creates, to some extent, a picture within a picture. The cathedral is set in space by positioning it so we see it through the frame of trees in the foreground. Constable has also used the old leaning trees to offset the Gothic perpendiculars of the architecture.

PAUL CÉZANNE
1839 • 1906

Paul Cézanne was born in Aix, a provincial town in southern France. He enrolled in art school against the wishes of his father, a tyrannical figure who hoped his son would study law. In his early twenties, Cézanne joined his boyhood friend Émile Zola in Paris. If in Aix, his countrymen called his art "clumsy and amateurish," in Paris, his "violent and aggressive" early paintings of rape and murder were considered to be in bad taste. He was the ultimate outsider, no matter where he lived.

Although Cézanne is remembered for his sensitive treatment of landscape, in his early years as a painter he was indifferent to this subject, and produced large figurative works. Cézanne often painted family members, including his mistress and later-to-be wife Marie-Hortense Figuet. He spent the majority of his career in search of an elusive goal – to find a perfect balance between nature and art.

LA MONTAGNE SAINTE-VICTOIRE (1905) by Paul Cézanne

This is a later version of many paintings Cézanne made of this mountain. By taking some of the colors from the foreground and using them in the sky Cézanne was trying to make us aware of the flat surface of the canvas. Although the sky and the mountain are painted strongly, there is no doubt about the recession across the ground away from the spectator to the base of the mountain. Every tiny part of the canvas is treated with great intensity.

SELF-PORTRAIT by Paul Cézanne

From the artist's appearance, this self-portrait is thought to have been painted in about 1880, by which time he had developed an individual set of color theories and painting techniques. Cézanne carefully considered and monitored the layers of overlaid color and small, obvious brush strokes used for large-scale hatching.

No other artist used color more passionately or innovatively than Cézanne. He took the choppy brush strokes of the Impressionist painters and gave them a structure, solidity, and permanence. Some of his most famous works include his more than 60 views of *Mont Sainte-Victoire*, various views of bathers, still lifes, and portraits.

When drawing figures Cézanne would consider the torso as a solid volume comprised of a surface structure of many different flat planes, rather than as a ribcage with muscle and skin stretched over it. Although this is an over-simplification, there is no doubt that Cézanne's attitude toward the depiction of the human figure was quite different in concept from that of previous artists.

Throughout his life Cézanne was obsessed by the theme of bathers. His early studies, which he made directly from the model, were coarse and frequently erotic. He attacked the canvas with great ferocity, laying on the paint in thick slashes with a pallet knife. His unconventional approach to drawing prevented him from ever fulfilling his ambition to paint more academic nudes after the fashion of the painter Delacroix.

Paul Cézanne was considered the greatest master of still life. He found that the form allowed him to concentrate on such fundamental problems as form and space and the paradox of transferring the three-dimensional world to a two-dimensional surface. Cézanne defined form and structure by an infinite variation of tone and space by the use of well regulated receding planes. If the underlying geometric structure sometimes makes his work appear severe, then the subtle variation of line and tone lends it a lyricism that has been admired and emulated ever since.

By the end of the 19th century Cézanne was a lonely and suspicious man, almost a recluse, although he still traveled to Paris quite regularly. In 1895, Pissarro suggested to Monet and Renoir that they encourage the young dealer Vollard to see what their friend from earlier days had been doing. The result was an exhibition of over 100 of Cézanne's paintings. Cézanne's friends, Degas included, bought as much as they could afford. He died in 1906 amidst a growing interest in his work but after the years of isolated innovation, he never believed his paintings were properly understood.

STILL LIFE WITH PITCHER by Paul Cézanne

Even when left unfinished, Cézanne's paintings and drawings have a completeness about them – every brush mark serves a purpose. Cézanne allowed the white ground of the canvas to form an integral part of the total composition. The artist also took great care in the actual placement of the objects before he began painting a still life.

VINCENT VAN GOGH
1839 • 1906

DETAIL OF DR. GACHET by Vincent van Gogh

Van Gogh has exploited the descriptive character of his brush strokes to emphasize the forms of the face, including the nose, cheekbones, and eyebrows. The marks of the bristle brush are often apparent in the thick paint and give an actual raised texture to the painting. The lively techniques and van Gogh's particular vision combine to create this intelligent, bright-eyed portrait.

Vincent van Gogh was born in Groot-Zundert, Netherlands, son of a small town preacher. He began his working life employed by Groupil & Cie, an international art dealer, but then left to consider a career with the church as his religious zeal grew. In 1879, having grown disenchanted with both formal religious education and the evangelist path, he decided to become an artist. Over the course of the next ten years, before he took his own life, he produced an enormous body of work. While it is not quite true that he never sold a piece of art, during his lifetime his primary supporters were his brother Theo and other artists. Van Gogh also relied on Theo for financial support. While some art historians question how much of van Gogh's current popularity is due to romantic mythology around the "insane genius," his work is unquestionably powerful and unique.

The paintings of van Gogh were dedicated to making people think and to bring them to understand the comfort and warmth of love. He wanted to express through his paintings the universal power of light. He learned from the Old Masters and from the Impressionists, but eventually developed his own style, working from the observation of real things and real people, in a highly subjective manner. He simplified form and exaggerated the drawing and the color. The warmth of his emotions and his reaction to the wonders of nature are expressed by his vibrant use of orange to represent sunlight. Like the Impressionists, he was fond of using complementary colors and found that he could set one off against the other to further intensify the emotional content.

Van Gogh's treatment of the human figure was one of sympathy and passion. His own anguish and suffering, which led to his eventual suicide, were expressed in his paintings as a feeling of isolation.

SELF PORTRAIT
by Vincent van Gogh

HENRI MATISSE
1869 • 1954

Henri Émile Benoît Matisse a French artist and a leader of the Fauve group, was regarded as one of the great formative figures in 20th-century art. He was a master of the use of color and form to convey emotional expression. Matisse studied contemporary art, especially that of the Impressionists, and he began to experiment, earning a reputation as a rebellious member of his studio classes.

Matisse's true artistic liberation, in terms of the use of color to render forms and organize spatial planes, came about first through the influence of the French painters Paul Gauguin and Paul Cézanne and the Dutch artist Vincent van Gogh, whose work he studied closely beginning about 1899. Then, in 1903 and 1904, Matisse encountered the Pointillist painting of Henri Edmond Cross and Paul Signac.

STUDY FOR PINK NUDE (1935) by Henri Matisse

This charcoal sketch demonstrates Matisse's marvelous sense of rhythmic line and form. Rubbed tone emphasizes the rounded forms while highlights are created by erasing certain areas.

LANDSCAPE AT COLLIOURE (1906) by Henri Matisse

Matisse tried for a short while to make his color schemes conform to the theories of some of his Post-Impressionist contemporaries, but his exuberant approach expressed itself more easily by intuition. The freedom with which he applied color to the canvas is deceptive; he composed his pictures with great care.

Cross and Signac were experimenting with juxtaposing small strokes (often dots or points) of pure pigment to create the strongest visual vibration of intense color. Matisse adopted their technique and modified it repeatedly, using broader strokes. By 1905 he had produced some of the boldest color images ever created.

Matisse had a high regard for Oriental art and was concerned with the concept of simplicity. He painted his figures in simple lines and flat colors, often using a single color to give a great intensity of mood. He saw costume as a way of introducing ornamental pattern, although his aim was not simply to decorate but to express life itself.

In his later paintings he became almost obsessed by the nude figure although he retained the individual decorative quality of his paintings by setting them against brightly colored backgrounds. His *Pink Nude*, which was painted in 1935, moved close to total abstraction, a style of art which greatly excited Matisse.

Matisse died in Nice on November 3, 1954. Unlike many artists, he was internationally popular during his lifetime, enjoying the favor of collectors, art critics, and the younger generation of artists.

PABLO PICASSO
1881 • 1973

SEATED WOMAN IN A CHEMISE (1923) by Pablo Picasso

The monumentality and calm grandeur of this figure almost gives it the appearance of classical sculpture. The angle of view helps to produce this effect as does the relative distortion of the hands and head. Another equally important element is the clothing – nominally a chemise, the thin drapery is arranged and depicted in such a way as to bring to mind the coverings of classical figures.

It was in Malaga on the southern Mediterranean coast of Spain that Pablo Picasso was born on October 25, 1881. It was here that he gained his first knowledge of the arts from his father, José Ruiz Blasco, an academic painter of average talent. When still a child, Pablo showed a remarkable ability to draw and amuse his friends by quick sketches that already went beyond the imaginative innocence of childhood.

In 1895 the family moved to Barcelona, which is where the young Pablo began to assert his independence and found friends among the avant-garde poets, painters and philosophers who frequented the famous *Els Quatre Gats* tavern.

LES DEMOISELLES D'AVIGNON

In his early years of painting, Picasso was interested by particular types of dress. He made paintings of Pierrots and Harlequins, often contrasting the gaiety of dress with the apparent melancholy of the model – the sad clown image.

Picasso developed the style of Cubism along with Georges Braque (1882–1963). This style became, in its final stage, a mixture of drawing, painting, and collage. The Cubist method of treating the composition as an arrangement of geometrically shaped planes related to the rectangular plane of the picture, was a clear influence on abstract art. However, Picasso and Braque never lost interest in the human figure as a source of inspiration, even when their fascination with abstraction grew.

Picasso treated the backgrounds of his Cubist paintings in the same way as the figures. The form is fragmented and so is space, making it difficult for the observer to translate. But Picasso does provide visual clues that help the viewer to recognize his familiar environment in the painting. In *Les Demoiselles d'Avignon* the figures are surrounded by what, at first, seem to be incomprehensible shapes. Then at the bottom of the canvas is a small still-life of fruit – a melon, pears and grapes. Suddenly the figures seem to be enclosed by folds of drapery, which are perhaps curtains. The eye and brain demand meaning from the visual work and where something is not fully explained, the imagination takes over.

It will be many years before the significance and greatness of Picasso can be truly assessed.

SUBJECTS

The first part of the book may have encouraged you to try out some techniques you had perhaps been nervous of in the past — or possibly had never heard of. The aim of this section is to show how the "craft" of painting is used by other artists. I have chosen seven main themes — still life, flowers, light and weather, water, buildings, the animal world, and portrait and figure work — and a wide variety of different approaches is shown in each of these subject areas.

Many of these themes are accompanied by a step-by-step demonstration in which you can follow an individual artist's progress from the conception of an idea to the completion of a painting. Remember to never feel inferior if you cannot paint exactly like them — instead, concentrate on your own personal style.

STILL LIFE

STILL LIFE FOR JUDY by Kay Gallwey

One of the most attractive aspects of still-life painting is that it is controllable. With a landscape you take the subject as it is, making only minor improvements on nature, if any. And there is always the worry that the sun will go in or come out; it may

suddenly pour with rain before you have finished; the shadows that formed an important part of the composition may change in shape and color, and so on. But with a still life you can choose the objects you like, decide where and how to arrange them, and take as long as you like over the picture.

At least in theory – in practice it is not quite so simple. If you decide to use natural light for the group (see lighting) you will encounter the same difficulties as the landscape painter – interior light can change very suddenly and dramatically. And, of course, if your subject is flowers, fruit, or vegetables they will wilt, shrivel, or ripen so that by the end of a week your still life may be very different from the one you first chose.

Cézanne, who painted some of the most marvelous still lifes ever seen, is reputed to have used artificial fruit for this reason – he painted very slowly. This is an idea worth considering; the silk flowers made nowadays, for instance, are both realistic and beautiful, and for a mixed group including one or two blooms they could be the perfect solution.

No branch of painting is problem free, and it is still true to say that still life offers an opportunity to practice your technique and try out your ideas in a highly enjoyable way. You can work quietly by yourself with no one looking over your shoulder, and even if you are not happy with the result the first time you will have learned something for the future.

YOUR CHOICES

The first thing you have to decide – and perhaps the most difficult – is what to paint. Novices have a tendency to look around the house and seize a random selection of objects, usually far too many, which does not usually make for a good picture.

So think about what your interests are. Perhaps you want to experiment with color combinations, in which case you might try some blue flowers in a blue jug, perhaps with a pink tablecloth for contrast, or a blue bowl full of oranges, which would provide an exciting exercise in complementaries. It is always best to restrict the colors and choose one dominant one; if you have too many they will fight with one another and the picture will be disjointed.

If you are more concerned with textures, on the other hand, a group consisting of fruit, glass, wood, and metal and perhaps some fabric would provide an interesting set of contrasts, as well as testing your technique and observational powers.

There is no reason why you should not be able to make an exciting painting out of nothing more elaborate than a few bottles, mugs, or jugs if shapes interest you more than either color or texture. Whatever you choose to paint there should be a definite motive behind it so that a kind of theme runs through the picture.

GRANDMOTHER'S
DOLLS by Barbara Willis

A still life often has one main object, which must be placed in a position of prominence with the other elements orchestrated around it. It should not usually be placed right in the middle, and here the doll's face is slightly off-center, with the circle of the hat proclaiming it as the center of attention.

ARRANGING THE GROUP

A still life should always have some sort of theme running through it. The culinary theme, of fruit, vegetables, and kitchen equipment, is a favorite one, as is garden and greenhouse articles. Because the objects are related through association they form the basis of a naturally harmonious picture.

Another type of theme is the biographical or narrative one, in which personal belongings such as shoes or a chair are depicted – van Gogh (1853–1890) painted both at different stages of his career.

A theme can also be purely visual, with objects chosen specifically for their shapes or colors. Plates and bowls on a table, for example, provide an arrangement of circles and horizontals (or diagonals), while bottles comprise a series of uprights and curves. A color theme could take the form of predominantly blue, white, or yellow objects. In van Gogh's famous *Sunflowers* the background, vase, and flowers are all shades of yellow.

Arranging a collection of objects so that they make a pleasing composition is one of the hardest aspects of still life painting, so be prepared to take time at this stage. You might begin by depositing the objects at random, perhaps even without looking. Then look at them through a viewing frame and adjust them until you begin to see a satisfactory composition that has both balance and a sense of movement.

You don't want an overstatic arrangement; the eye should always be led from one part of the picture to another, and you need to establish a pictorial relationship between the objects. This can sometimes be done by overlapping, allowing one object to cast a shadow on another or by placing some drapery so that it curves between, behind and/or in front of the various elements. The latter is a commonly used device in still life painting, and oddly enough it seldom looks artificial.

Circles (fruit or plates) and other regular geometric shapes are useful as eye-catchers, and often form good focal points. Be careful how you place straight lines, as the eye automatically travels along them. Diagonals and verticals, such as those formed by the front edge and legs of a table placed at an angle, are excellent for leading the eye in to a focal point, but parallel horizontals are best avoided as they have a blocking effect.

ORANGES AND GILD BOX by Pamela Kay

A common mistake when setting up a group is including too many shapes and colors, resulting in patchy and incoherent paintings in which all the diverse elements vie for attention. If you do opt for an elaborate group, you will have to devise a means of uniting the various components in pictorial terms, as the artist has done in the painting above. There are a lot of shapes and colors, but the picture has a marvelous unity because each one has an echo in another part of the painting.

STILL LIFE WITH FRUIT by Hazel Harrison

The light source, coming from the left, casts shadows that break up the background and cause reflected highlights on the glass. Since glass is transparent it is not illuminated on one side only, as a solid object is, and most of what we see is a distorted image of whatever is behind the glass. The fruit and plate in this picture are the only forms that are strongly modeled from light to dark.

LIGHTING

A group of inanimate objects illuminated solely by artificial light will stay the same indefinitely. This is ideal for the painter who wants to practice technique without feeling rushed. Special bulbs, which simulate natural light quite well, can now be bought in most art shops, but the real thing is usually best as it reflects a greater range of colors and casts stronger shadows.

The most dramatic still lifes are those that are lit directly by the sun so that strong shadows fall across the subject and below the objects, accentuating their forms and colors. If you opt for this kind of painting you will have to work in a series of sessions; never fall prey to the temptation of changing your painting as the sun moves around.

WILD POSY by Juliette Palmer

Back lighting can be particularly effective for still lifes, as can be seen from this dramatic painting. It has made the petals glow dramatically, with the fine hairs bordering the stems catching the light to create a delicate silhouette. The dark, spiky shadow creates exciting foreground interest and balances the strong shapes above.

It is a good idea to try out several different natural light effects before making the final decision. You can do this by choosing one or two key objects from your group and turning them around so that the light falls first on the front and then on either side. You will probably notice that front lighting is the least interesting; it is usually avoided in both still lifes and portraits because it has a flattening effect.

Back lighting can be extremely effective for some subjects, as it partially silhouettes the forms and haloes their edges. A potted plant or vase of flowers on a windowsill can be transformed by the light behind it, which shines through some leaves and petals and casts dark shadows on others. Again, this would call for a series of short working sessions or a very rapid *alla prima* approach.

BACKGROUNDS

The background is just as important as any other part of a still life, and should never be treated just as an area where nothing is happening. It is akin to the sky in a landscape, and may even comprise a greater proportion of the canvas surface than the objects themselves. With a flat background it can be more satisfactory to block in all the parts of the picture together but complete the final painting of the background after and around the other objects. In this way the shapes between objects are truly observed and stated with conviction.

It also gives you a chance to sharpen up and redefine the edges of the objects, and ensures that the brushwork has equal prominence in all areas of the picture.

At the setting-up stage, experiment with a variety of tablecloths, curtains, pieces of furniture, or plain walls. It is important that the objects harmonize with the background in terms of color and are not swamped.

Plain backgrounds can work very well as long as they are not painted too flatly, so try to keep the colors lively, perhaps by painting over a colored ground or using broken color, scumbling, or glazing.

GOLDEN SPLENDOUR by Sid Willis

Here the glorious silk fabrics in foreground and background are the dominant features, and were obviously the main reason for painting the picture. Nevertheless, the brass pot, high in the picture, is the focal point, and the dark red cloth behind has been cleverly darkened and muted in color so that it recedes and creates a sense of space. The execution of the whole work is stunning, with every crease and fold in the cloths lovingly observed and every reflection in the pot faithfully included.

An elaborate or patterned background can act as a foil for plain objects, but another approach is to continue a pattern on a vase, say, across the picture plane by a similar wallpaper or curtain. This decorative treatment was used by Henri Matisse (1869–1954), who was more interested in color and pattern than in the description of form.

CHRISTMAS ROSES BY Christopher Baker

Plain dark backgrounds have traditionally been used for floral groups, and here near-black shows off the delicacy of the roses to perfection. Notice that there is almost no visible division between the dark table top and the background itself, so that nothing competes with the flowers and glass, the latter owing its visibility entirely to a few reflections and highlights.

LE BONHEUR DE VIVRE (The Joy of Life) by Henri Matisse (1905-1906)

Matisse pursued the expressiveness of color throughout his career and his art has an astonishing force.

FLORAL STILL LIFE STEP-BY-STEP

1 Although the arrangement is a simple one it was given careful consideration before the painting began. The plant was placed on the tablecloth and rotated until it provided the most interesting configuration of flowers.

2 The artist began by making a careful underdrawing, noting the positions of the flowers in relation to each other. Because the flowers are basically white, he chose to block in the dark background first.

3 Next the artist mixes the colors for the petals. To make sure that the color is correct, the artist holds the brush up close to the petals and adjusts the mixture until he is satisfied with the match. This is a useful way of analyzing colors – most people have a tendency to paint what they think should be there rather than what really is. It also enables you to establish a tonal key for the painting.

4 The mixed color is now applied. Since few petals are exactly the same color, repeated alterations of the paint mixture are required as work progresses. Before completing the petals, some of the foliage, especially the darkest areas, is painted.

5 The yellow flower centers and the pot provide some warm colors in a predominantly cool picture.

6 After completing the tablecloth area, the shapes of the most important leaves – those that stand out against the background – are defined with a sable brush.

7 This detail shows that the "white" petals range in color from yellowish whites through pinks to fairly dark purplish grays. Many of these color variations are caused by the angles at which the petals lie to the light source.

The little patches of blues and ochers in the background provide additional interest while also helping it to recede by setting up a "shimmer" effect. These patches were initially too clear cut and bright, so were tonked (see pages 52–53) with newspaper.

FLOWERS

For the beginner, flowers and their foliage provide an endless source of subject matter to practice on in any medium, even if you do not intend to specialize in them. From wild flowers to exotic, cultivated varieties, there is always something to paint, even in the dead of winter. They are also a good subject for the disabled or those who are housebound. Even if you have never drawn a flower before, this section will show you how to make a start.

Flowers have been symbolic through the ages: life and death, the seasons, and your emotions can all be depicted through flowers. Artists use flowers and leaves for the message they can give, telling a story or sending a wish to a friend. For example, ivy is a fairly universal symbol for friendship or fidelity, and a red rose has the obvious implications of love. During the Renaissance, Mary, the mother of Jesus, was invariably painted with a white lily, the symbol of purity – this gave rise to the name, Madonna lily.

Most great artists have depicted flowers in some form or other. In the seventeenth and eighteenth centuries, Dutch painters were renowned for their rich, glowing flower portraits. These depicted wonderfully elaborate arrangements, with meticulous attention given to a shining dewdrop or a snail, added to give emphasis to the composition. The fact that all the flowers in one painting could not have been in season at the same time does not seem to have mattered – perhaps the artists painted in each flower as it appeared through the seasons. The rich colors and gorgeous displays gave the Dutch pride of place in the flower-painting world, and this work is well represented in many major collections.

COLOR CHOICES

The brilliant colors of flowers may tempt you to buy a huge range of paints, but it is better to start with the smallest number you can and practice color mixing.

You may in time find you need some special "flower colors," because mixing more than two or three colors can cause a loss of clarity, but these can be purchased as the need arises.

It is essential to have two or three different reds, yellows, and blues. These are called the primary colors because they cannot be produced by mixing other colors. Choosing a crimson (slightly blue) red and a more brilliant one such as cadmium red, will help you mix the different pinks and purples. A good orange (cadmium for example) is useful as it can be difficult to mix. Some artists maintain all greens should be mixed from various combinations of blue and yellow, but most palettes include at least one green.

Titanium white   Ivory black

Cadmium yellow   Chrome yellow

Indian yellow   Cadmium orange

Phthalo blue   Dioxine purple

Permanent rose   Permanent mauve

Permanent magenta   Mars brown

SHAPE AND STRUCTURE

You do not need to be a botanist to paint flowers, but understanding their basic structures will avoid frustration and help you depict them successfully.

You would not draw a figure without considering the muscles and bones that form it and the way the feet and legs support he body's weight. The same applies to a plant. For example, the stem must be strong enough to support the flower. It is unlikely to be thinner at the bottom or it could not support the weight above. If a long leaf seems to bend over, as they often do, it must still have a logical progression with no broken lines for the veins.

Many flowerheads can be simplified into a basic circle, and when a circle is seen in perspective, turned away from

you, it becomes an ellipse. Practice drawing ellipses as they are the magic formula for solving a number of problems that beset the beginner. Hold a saucer up and look at it full face, imagine it is a daisy and turn it slowly on its axis so that it is flat. Just for fun, as it is a very loose analogy, lightly draw the saucer on three or four different planes and then put it down and turn its shape into a flower – a simple daisy.

Think about what happens when the basic shape is broken. For example, if your saucer of a daisy had a limp petal hanging down on one side and you pushed it back into place, it would fit back into the ellipse; it would not have become longer or thinner, though it might look that way. Perspective and foreshortening need to be observed carefully, and the various angles can be worked out in a

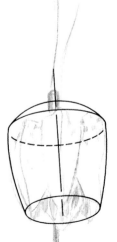

BELL-SHAPED

Flowers of this type follow the three-dimensional shape of a bell; the stem supports the flower from the center top, the petals fall around the axis of the stamen, which corresponds to the clapper. The shadow is deep on the inside, and there may be a curve of light to the back, inner edge.

TRUMPET-SHAPED

A lily, with its stamens protruding out like symbols of noise, makes an obvious trumpet. Many other tubular flowers start conical and then the petals flare into the familiar trumpet shape. Make sure that the petals curve into a center point, even when they disappear into shade.

MULTI-HEADED

Look for the overall shape of the whole cluster of flowers, a ball, cone, or something more irregular. Work out the planes of each individual flower and pay most attention to the detail of the nearest ones to you, leaving the ones away from the light source to dissolve in shadow.

SPIKE-SHAPED

Even quite large flowered spikes, such as gladioli, can form an overall cone, so treat them as one shape. Note the central line of the stem and how the flowers surround it. Tackle the shading as a whole. For any close-ups, let the brushwork indicate the individual flowers rather than painting in each one.

separate drawing with guide lines made obvious.

More complex flowers, where the basic shape is not obvious, require more acute observation, but the principles are the same. If you do not understand how or why a shape is as it is, take one flower apart very gently and slowly and see how it is put

together. Look at the different stages and see whether an older flower has the start of a seed pod developing. This sounds obvious, but for a spray on a single stem you will need to show the progression from the wide open flower at the bottom to the bud at the top.

BASIC LEAF SHAPES

The shape of the leaf identifies the plant as much as the flowers. The subtle differences of shapes are particularly important where the color of the flower is matched – deep red flowers may be supported by a leaf tinged with maroon, while the same genus carrying a white flower may show a paler green leaf.

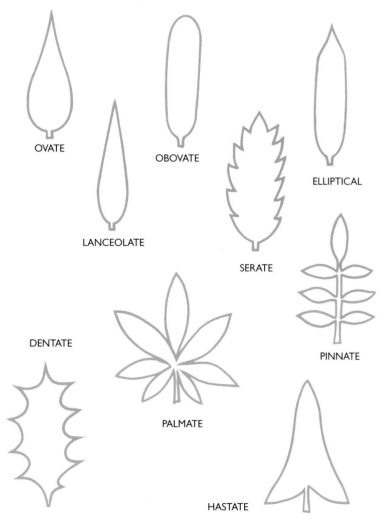

OVATE

LANCEOLATE

OBOVATE

SERATE

ELLIPTICAL

DENTATE

PALMATE

PINNATE

HASTATE

ARRANGING FLOWERS

You need not become an expert florist overnight to paint flowers, but a brief explanation of the basic principles of flower arranging may come in useful.

The more formal arrangements follow well-defined rules, however uncontrived they may look. A florist usually builds the outline starting with the foliage. The height and width are fixed first, with "anchor" stems that form a triangle marking the outside limits and creating the required shape and size. No stems should ever cross and each should be angled to a central vanishing point in your mind, even if it is well below the vase in reality. Every piece of foliage and flowerhead is likewise worked in triangles. The central front, lowest point, is placed next, and the left and right centers of each side, forming another triangle. Then the flowers can be put in, working around in the same order, making triangles with the longest points.

Color and value become the next concern. Pale colors need to be placed with care as they draw the eye to the shape. Ideally start with a spray of small white or pale flowers as the second highest point and continue it through to one side, making that the second longest point. Then do the same with another type of light flower but running through to the opposite side to balance it. Blues will recede and yellows come forward when viewed from a distance. Red, although theoretically an advancing color, can be deceptive and may not be as attention grabbing as you imagine. If it is the deepest shade it will certainly recede; it is only when yellow is added and it becomes orange that it starts to take over. Always reserve three large blooms or dense-shaped flowers to give depth to the center of the display, pushed well down into the arrangement toward the final stages, forming another triangle. All flower arrangements use odd numbers of stems, threes, fives, and sevens, and are based on exaggerations of these principles.

CONTAINERS AND VASES

The container should obey the same laws of gravity as in real life. It should not appear as though it will keel over under the weight of the mass it holds. Your painting may not show a great deal of it as it may be covered with flowers and foliage, but it must still provide a solid foundation for the rest of the painting.

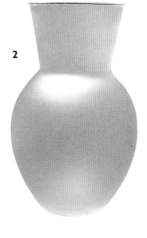

The container must take the weight of flowers without falling over, and empathize stylistically.
1 *A tall, slender vase is ideal for long stems.*
2 *A rounded, pearlized vase sets off pale colors and round flowers.*
3 *A tall, strongly colored jug complements gladioli and strong flowers.*
4 *A solid, plain jug suggests cornflowers or nigella and daisies.*

DAFFODILS: STEP-BY-STEP

Oil paints, although perhaps not quite so versatile as acrylics, can be used in a variety of ways and adapted to many different methods. The artist has evolved a personal and highly individual way of working, which involves using very thin, runny paint for the background, and applying the colors for the flowers with pieces of mount board, each one cut to the right size for the job. He also uses painting knives for small details and fine lines and for sgraffito (scratching paint away).

1 The background was laid with a very broad household brush dipped first into white spirit and then into a diluted mixture of purple and blue. He works into the paint with a roller while still wet to give it texture.

3 With the background color still slightly wet, he begins to lay on thicker paint for the flowers, using the piece of board like a spatula. The yellow does not completely cover the blue, creating a shadow effect on the petals. With more of the flowers laid in, the point of a painting knife is used to scratch lines into the still-wet yellow paint, revealing the blue beneath. The background color has to be dry for this method.

2 With the paint still wet, he uses a piece of mount board to "lift out" the shapes of the flowers, making the long, thin lines with the edge. It is important to cut the edge perfectly straight, so that it makes full contact with the surface.

4 For the stems, the whole length of the card is used. The paint is placed with the edge of the card, and then dragged a little sideways to give the width of the stem. The artist wants to avoid too much emphasis on the vase and tabletop, so he treats this area as an interplay of abstract shapes, pulling a lighter blue downward and sideways so that it partially obscures part of the vase.

5 In the final stages, some further detail was built up on the flowers with the painting knife, and a large, flat brush is used to tidy up areas of the background behind the flowers.

6 The impact of this painting stems from its simplicity. The artist's interest was in the silhouette shapes of the light-colored flowers and dark jug against the mid-toned background, and he has deliberately avoided any detail that might dilute his pictorial message.

GERANIUM: STEP-BY-STEP

1 Because these flowers are not intricate in shape and do not have a wealth of small detail to record, you can take a painterly approach to them, but you do want to be able to blend the colors well to show the soft gradations. You can do it with oil paints used at a fairly sloppy consistency. Start by laying on the darkest color, around the edges of the petals where they curve away from the light, and in the centers.

2 Do not add more paint yet. Instead, before the color has begun to dry, take a clean brush and drag it down so that it spreads out more thinly in the center of each petal, allowing the white of the canvas to show through.

3 Work the other flower in the same way, then add a band of light brown to the leaf, blending it in with a dry brush or your finger, and finally paint in the leaf and flower veins with a small brush.

LIGHT AND WEATHER

The ability to generate a feeling of atmosphere and mood in a landscape painting is one of the hallmarks of a skilled artist. The prevailing light and weather conditions play an important part in establishing such a mood, and will often turn a perfectly ordinary scene into a memorable one. Strong sunlight makes the very air vibrate with color and gives rise to deep, dark shadows. Fog and mist act like a veil upon the landscape, turning hills and trees into eerie shapes that seem to float above the land. Storm clouds are particularly dramatic, especially when strong shafts of sunlight break through and spotlight the distant landscape. Lashing wind and rain set the landscape in motion as trees bend and leaves fly. After a fall of snow, the whole landscape seems hushed and still, the dark shapes of trees and buildings looming in stark contrast to the whiteness of the land.

Though it is possible to recreate atmospheric effects from photographs, there is no substitute for actually getting out there among the elements. Other senses apart from sight have a part to play in painting; if you can smell the sun on the grass, hear the pounding of surf against the rocks, or feel the sharpness of a frosty day, these qualities will come through in your painting, almost without your being aware of it. Even in a blizzard or a downpour, it is possible to work directly from nature by viewing the scene from your car window, or finding some other shelter. If you can't actually set up your easel, weather conditions can be recorded quickly in a watercolor or pencil sketch, so that a finished painting can be painted later in the studio. Indeed, working under adverse conditions often forces you to work directly and spontaneously, capturing the essence of the weather without danger of overworking your painting.

When painting the weather, it is important to switch off the analytical side of your brain and be responsive to the feelings generated by a sparkling spring day or a crashing thunderstorm. Because atmospheric conditions are transitory and difficult to "pin down," the creative artist turns this to advantage by letting the paint itself suggest the power and drama of nature.

FOG AND MIST

A landscape that is shrouded in mist takes on a strange, haunting, unfamiliar aspect, and this indefinable quality has attracted artists for centuries. The great masters of traditional Chinese and Japanese paintings delighted in rendering, with a few exquisite brush strokes, an impression of mountains and trees looming out of the mist. Of the European painters, Turner is the

SNOW STORM: HANNIBAL AND HIS ARMY CROSS THE ALPS by J. M. W. Turner (1812)

This imaginative composition shows a mixture of romanticism and worldliness. The dramas of nature form the real subject, and Turner no doubt enjoyed the irony that the soldiers survived the passage only to suffer a more tedious defeat in Italy.

unequaled master of depicting the effects of sun, water, and light on landscapes and seascapes.

Because fog and mist are actually water vapor hanging in the air, it follows that a fluid medium such as watercolor lends itself particularly well to such a subject. Oil paints can be used with great success, because their slow rate of drying allows for subtle wet-in-wet blendings.

Fog acts as a filter on the landscape, reducing forms to simple silhouettes, minimizing tonal contrast, and eliminating textural detail. There are many techniques that you can use

to render this effect in your paintings. In oils, an excellent method is to apply a toned ground of heavily diluted raw umber and then to render the muted tones and colors of the landscape with delicate scumbles that allow the ground color to show through. This technique produces a highly atmospheric, soft focus effect.

Another interesting technique is to tonk the painting with newspaper before the paint dries. This removes much of the color from the surface and has an overall softening effect on the painting.

WEATHER IN LANDSCAPE

The appearance of the landscape on any particular day – or even minute – is governed by the weather, indeed the weather in many cases *is* the landscape, and can form a subject for painting in its own right. For instance, everyone has seen a sunny, tranquil view becoming dark and brooding as a storm brews up, or watched a dull landscape being transformed into a place of magic by a gleam of sunlight emerging through mist or rain.

Such effects, however, are fleeting, so get into the habit of making small on-the-spot sketches that you can use as a basis for studio paintings (you can also use photographs, but try not to rely on them too heavily).

Both Constable (1776–1837) and Turner (1775–1851) were fascinated by weather effects, and made countless small, color notes of this kind. Constable was particularly interested in rainbows, which offer a marvelous opportunity to contrast bright colors with a mass of dark grays.

Pouring rain seldom makes an interesting subject, but light rain sometimes does, particularly when gleams of light are visible. Mist creates lovely atmospheric effects, softening

BRIGHTON BEACH by John Constable

To achieve the shifting flicker of light and weather Constable abandoned fine traditional finish, catching the sunlight in blobs of pure white or yellow, and the drama of storms with a rapid brush.

SEPTEMBER, WATERFORD MARSH by Trevor Chamberlain

The pastel shades of this misty scene have been achieved by using highly unsaturated colors –
that is those mixed with a substantial amount of white. Very careful control of tones is needed
for scenes like this, and it is wise to mix several colors side by side on the palette before putting
them onto the canvas. Alternatively, stronger colors can be applied and then given a misty veil
of white or gray, using either the dry brush or the glazing techniques. In this case the underlayer
of paint must be completely dry.

the contours of shapes and reducing the intensity of colors. You might find either the finger painting or the scraping back techniques useful here. For stormy skies, try to make your brushwork as lively and descriptive as possible. You can indicate falling rain by using diagonal or vertical brush strokes to build up the painting, or you can ignore the raindrops and choose instead to imply the effects of rain on the landscape by softly diffusing the images.

SKIES AND CLOUDS

The great theatrical effects of light and color in the sky have produced some of the most magnificent and sublime works in the history of art. Glorious sunsets, towering banks of sunlit cumulus cloud, dark, storm-filled skies, the feather patterns of cirrus clouds against a clear blue expanse: these are the kind of subjects that have attracted artists for generations. The great English landscape painter John Constable declared that "The sky is the source of light in nature and governs everything."

It is not always easy to know how to treat skies in terms of paint. A common mistake is to put on the paint for the sky much more flatly than elsewhere in the painting, with much use of blending methods, which seems to be the most logical means of expressing the insubstantial nature of air. However, it is essential to think as much about the painting as you do about the subject, and it will not hang together properly unless the brushwork is consistent throughout.

WARTIME by Albert Goodwin

Albert Goodwin conveys a powerful feeling of perspective and scale in this painting. See what a large expanse of the canvas is devoted to the broad mass of clouds that scud overhead and draw us into the picture.

MONT SAINTE-VICTOIRE by Paul Cézanne (1905–1906)

Cézanne made numerous studies of Mont Sainte-Victoire and this somber version was painted in the year of his death.

If you want a subtly blended sky with no visible brush marks – and there is nothing wrong with this – you must make sure to treat the land in the same way. On the other hand, if you are making a feature of brushwork you must carry it through the whole picture. When van Gogh depicted a clear blue sky he did so in swirling strokes of thick paint similar to those he used for the land, and in the landscapes of Cézanne the bold brush strokes are as evident in the sky as anywhere else.

The colors of clouds are often quite unexpected, as is their tonal range, so careful observation is needed. There are, however, some general guidelines that are useful to know if you find you have to re-create a sky from memory.

The color of a cloud depends primarily on the illumination it receives. At midday, when the sun is high, there will be little variety in the color, and the tops will be almost pure white. A low sun, for instance in the evening or on a winter day, casts a yellowish light, and the illuminated side of a cloud is distinctly yellow also. The other side, which is in shadow, can be bluish if it is reflecting clear sky or brownish if not.

The other factor which determines cloud color is distance. If you think of the sky as a wide, flat soup bowl inverted over your head you will realize that the clouds overhead are much further away from you than those on the horizon, and are thus affected by the laws of aerial perspective (see pages 105–107).

RECORDING SKIES

Dramatic skies and interesting cloud formations can be used in a compositional way to add extra interest to a landscape. Their shapes and colors can echo or complement features on the ground, such as hills or clumps of trees. However, clouds do present problems when you are working on location, as they are constantly forming, re-forming, moving around the sky, and sometimes disappearing altogether. It is hard to resist the temptation to make changes – each new formation seems better than the one before – which inevitably destroys the brushwork and overworks the paint. The best course is to work out your composition rapidly and then stick to it, putting small patches of color down all over the painting to relate the cloud colors to those of the land below.

In one way the changeability of cloud formations can be seen as an advantage, since if you watch them for a while you can choose the shapes best suited to your composition. It is not a bad idea to build up a "reference library" of cloud studies, as Constable did. Small oil sketches on paper can be made in a matter of minutes, and will teach you a great deal about the shapes, colors, and general behavior of clouds as well as providing material for later paintings.

RIVER TEST AT LECKFORD by William Garfit

THE BEACH by Andrew Macara

In this busy beach scene the artist has balanced passages of soft, neutral color with carefully distributed spots of vivid color. The neutral areas act as a foil for the bright colors, heightening their intensity by contrast.

BRIGHT SUNSHINE

When painting a scene bathed in bright sunshine, it is all too easy to become "blinded" by the intensity of color and light. The result is that the painting becomes too high in key overall, lacks tonal contrast, and generally looks washed out. Interestingly, the secret of creating the effect of bright sunlight lies in painting the shadows. Light looks even brighter when surrounded by darks, which is why many artists employ the

compositional device of throwing a shadow across the foreground and placing a small, brightly lit area in the middle ground. The viewer's eye instinctively focuses on that spot of bright light, and the scene looks sunny, even though most of it is in shadow. When the sun is at its most intense, the color of the light itself affects the local colors of the objects it strikes, often quite dramatically. Everything the sun hits becomes lighter and warmer in tone, while shadows are correspondingly cool because they reflect the blue of the sky. Balance bright, warm colors with deep, cool shadows so that they intensify each other and create strong value contrasts that spell "sunshine."

Another important point to watch out for is the reflected light in shadows. On a sunny day, there is so much light about that it bounces from one object to another. Thus, the shadow side of a white house may look blue, reflecting the sky, or it may be tinged with green if there are trees nearby. Being aware of subtle points like this will lend greater luminosity to your painting.

Brushwork techniques also contribute to the atmosphere of the painting. In opaque media, always paint the shadows thinly and use thick impasto (which reflects a lot of light) for painting light-valued areas. In watercolor, the bleaching effect of the sun is rendered simply and effectively by leaving white shapes for highlights. Remember also that intense sunlight diminishes sharp details, so use softened brushwork in some areas.

THE THREE GRACES by Charles Sovek

Note the broad handling of the paint here. Aside from the heads and hands there's very little detail, yet the impression of strong sunlight is very effective. There is a lot to be said for working quickly and spontaneously to catch the "first impression."

SHADOWS

Shadows are not always dramatic or threatening, they can introduce beauty and poetry to a painting. Most landscape painters prefer to work in the early morning or late afternoon, when the sun is at a low angle to the earth and trees and buildings cast long, descriptive shadows. A nice painting time is late afternoon on a sunny day in autumn, when everything is bathed in a soft, golden light and the lengthening shadows lend a magical air of calm and stillness to the scene.

When a cast shadow travels across another object that lies in its path, that object becomes much more interesting to look at. In addition to describing three-dimensional form, the graphic lines of shadows offer an interesting paradox – unconsciously we shift back and forth between seeing the shadows as a descriptive element and as a purely abstract pattern. In this way our imagination is fueled and we play an active part in the work.

It is useful to carry a sketchbook with you whenever you can and make visual notes of any interesting shadow patterns you come across. For example, those cast by a tree, or a wrought-iron gate, or the dappled shadows of trees and plants on a garden path.

THE INN COURTYARD by Roy Herrick

Even a corner of your own back garden can be transformed by the magic of shadows. Here the sun filters down through the leaves of the tree, casting a lace-like pattern of light and shadow across the pathway.

SNOW AND ICE

Snow and ice are generally regarded as being white, but they are in fact rarely pure white, except in the brightest areas. Snow and ice are water in solid form, and, just like water, they reflect color from the sky and nearby objects. This is especially noticeable in the early morning and late afternoon, when the sun strikes the surface of the snow at a low angle and tinges it a delicate pink or yellow. In fact, these are the best times of the day for painting snow scenes; the light is far lovelier than it is during the middle of the day, casting warm pinks and golds in the highlights, and luminous blues and violets in the shadows. In addition, the long shadows cast by the sun at these times of the day add drama to the scene and help to define the snow-covered forms of the land.

Inexperienced artists tend to think that painting a snow scene means piling on endless layers of thick white paint. On the contrary, the most atmospheric snow scenes are those that contain a lot of shadow, with only small areas of bright, sunlit snow. The bright spots look dazzling because of the contrasting shadows, whereas if the whole picture were painted in bright white the effect would be flat and monotonous, with no feeling of light at all.

When painting a snow scene in opaque media, always begin with the light colors and gradually add the cool shadow colors. It takes less paint to darken a light color than it does to lighten a dark color. With transparent watercolor, the opposite applies. You must establish the position of the brightest highlights on the snow in advance, and paint around them, working from light to dark.

After a heavy fall of snow, the objects that it covers take on soft contours and curves. The light planes blur softly into the shadow planes, with no hard edges, so model these forms with wet-in-wet blending.

When painting shadows on snow, you will notice that they appear crisp near the object casting the shadow, but more diffused farther away. This is because a lot of reflected light enters the shadows from the sky or from nearby snowdrifts. Keep the shadows airy and transparent by using thin pigment and fresh, clean color.

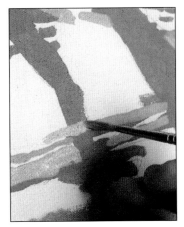

2 Then he adds the middle tones of the shadows, using a pale blue mixture.

1 Once the basic colors for the sky and hills have been laid in cerulean blue and white, the artist paints in the long shadows with a mixture of cerulean blue and a small amount of white and black.

3 As the painting develops the artist softens the hard lines of the snow and shadows by splattering white paint in the foreground to suggest falling snow.

4 In the finished picture the artist has successfully created dramatic contrasts using simple forms and a limited palette for the dark silhouetted trees against the sky, and the blue shadows against the snow.

187

WATER

Water is one of the most attractive of all painting subjects, partly because it is so appealing in itself. There can be few people who do not enjoy gazing at a peaceful expanse of lake or river mirroring the surrounding land, a shallow stream with its complex pattern of ripples, or the wild waves and spray of a stormy sea.

Because of its unique qualities, however, water does pose a challenge to the artist. It is transparent and yet has its own physical presence; it seems to reflect light in unpredictable ways; its patterns and colors are hard to analyze. The first thing to realize is that you cannot generalize about water, and the second is that to paint it successfully you will have to observe very closely so that you can learn to simplify.

WATER IN MOTION

This applies particularly to moving water. Transparent when you are close to it, a mirror when you are farther away, it takes on a very different appearance as it swirls around or tumbles over rocks, or swells to form breakers in the sea. At first, the task of capturing such movements in paint may seem daunting, but if you watch a stream, waterfall, or seascape for a time you will see that the movements follow a definite pattern, which is repeated again and again. Once you

understand this you will be able to paint with confidence, letting your brushwork describe the movement.

STILL WATER

On the face of it, painting a flat expanse of water seems easier, but there is a pitfall waiting for the unwary here. In beginner's paintings, water often appears to be flowing uphill, while in fact, of course, it is a flat horizontal plane and must be shown as such. If you paint it the same all over it will look like a wall, so you will have to find a way of suggesting recession. Putting in a few ripples or floating matter in the foreground is one way of doing this, and varying your brush strokes so that they are smaller in the distance is another.

COLOR

Clean water has no color of its own, allowing us, when we are close to it, to see through to whatever is below. In nature, however, water is seldom completely clean; it may contain suspended mud or vegetation that gives it a color of its own. Mountain streams, for instance, are often a lovely sherry-brown color because of the presence of peat in the water, while the algae in ponds or sluggish rivers can make the water distinctly green.

Because the surface of water is reflective, it also takes on color from the sky and surrounding land. If the water is still, it will show almost exactly the same colors as the sky above, but choppy water is a great deal less predictable. First, the movement of the water stirs up any suspended matter, and second, waves and ripples cast their own shadows so that parts of the water may appear surprisingly dark in relation to the sky.

TECHNIQUES

There is no one particular technique for rendering water. Although you might think that diluted paint or the wet into wet method will emulate the qualities of water, this is not always the case. Opaque paint can often be more successful if the painter takes care to place the colors accurately. In general, however, it is best to keep your brushwork broad and fluid, and avoid trying to describe every detail. Too much fiddling with a small brush tends to destroy both the impression of wetness and the sense of movement – most people must have noticed how photographs can "freeze" water and make it look solid and static.

THE DROWNING POOL by Nigel Casseldine

MOVING WATER

Painting fast-flowing water demands a keen eye and a sure hand. Once again, the trick is not to be overwhelmed by the apparent complexity of shadows and highlights. Look at the water through half-closed eyes and pick out the most obvious ripples and wavelets. Paint only these, with swift, decisive strokes.

To paint the rushing, white water of rapids and waterfalls, let the action of your brush suggest detail and movement. A few curving drybrush strokes, not too labored, are all that is needed to create an impression of water falling downward. Using a rough-textured paper or canvas helps, because the raised tooth of the surface catches and drags at the paint.

The patterns of waves, ripples, and reflections in water are a never-ending subject for study. It is a good idea to carry a sketchbook with you so that you can make on-the-spot studies of the form, direction, and movement of water in different situations and weather conditions.

In the step-by-step instructions on page 191 the artist is making a rapid oil sketch of the surface of a lake on a breezy day, when the water is ruffled by the wind and breaks up into tiny wavelets.

EVENING LIGHT, ARISAIG by David Curtis

1 Using a No. 4 flat bristle brush, the artist paints the dark ripples with curving strokes of Payne's gray and ultramarine.

2 With a mixture of ultramarine and white, criss-cross strokes are now blocked in for the lighter ripples, and the ruffled white highlights are put in last.

3 The paint is allowed to dry for about 15 minutes, then the artist blends the colors a little by brushing over the surface very lightly with a 1 in. (2.5 cm) decorator's brush.

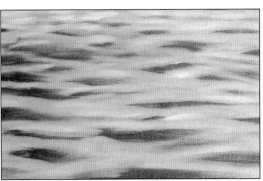

4 The finished study captures the impression of moving water which reflects the gray sky above.

REFLECTIONS

An important property of water is its ability to reflect light at its surface, thus acting as a mirror of the land or other features above. But it is vital to remember that the mirror in this case is a horizontal surface, and the strength of the reflection increases in proportion to the angle at which you view it. If you are standing at the edge of a lake and looking down at the water at your feet you will see little but the sand, stones, or mud below the surface, but if you look at the distant shore you will see a clear reversed image of the landscape behind the lake.

The rules of reflections are often misunderstood, but in fact they are always exactly the same height as the objects that cast them. However near or far from you it is, the reflection of a boat will be the same size as the boat itself, a useful rule to bear in mind when re-creating from memory or sketches.

Choppy water, of course, plays

BOATS AT BALMAHA by Peter Graham

Built on a color key of blue, purple, and red, this striking painting owes much of its feeling of movement to the swirling reflections. Although Graham seldom translates colors literally, he has ensured that the colors of the reflections are consistent with the features being reflected.

tricks with the rules, breaking up reflections and scattering them sideways or downward. This is because the horizontal surface has been broken up into a number of inclined, or even near-vertical planes. You will need to observe such effects very carefully, as each wave or ripple will be reflecting more than one color. Always try to simplify when you come to paint, as overworking water subjects is a recipe for failure. Broken reflections are usually adequately represented by interspersing horizontal patches of color.

ABOVE: THE SPADE AND BUCKET
by James Horton

It is not always easy to make the ripples in water look natural, but the mistake most often made is that of overworking. Here the choppy water with its broken reflections is beautifully conveyed through a series of separate brush strokes, each one laid down with precision and then left alone. It is often easier to work wet on dry for this kind of effect, as this allows the marks of the brush to remain crisp and clean, without mingling with an earlier layer of paint.

BELOW: CARP FISHING, SHIREOAKS
by David Curtis

The smooth, still water faithfully mirrors the buildings, trees, and sky, though a few small ripples break the symmetry.

THE SEA

Seascapes are an irresistible subject – to paint or simply to sit and look at – but they are not always easy to depict convincingly. One of the difficulties is, of course, their changeable nature: even quite minor alterations in weather conditions will produce a completely new set of the colors, while a calm sea will suddenly be transformed by a rising wind.

If you normally work on a large scale but want to paint on the spot it is wise to restrict yourself to small sketches. You can make several in the course of a day and these can be used as the basis for a studio painting later on.

The most important decision is deciding on the viewpoint and composition. A beach will present two extremes of choice, one looking along the shoreline so that the beach and the sea form wedges as they recede into the distance, and the other looking straight out to sea with the shoreline and horizon crossing the picture plane horizontally. In the latter case you will have to decide where to place the horizon. It should not be directly in the middle, as this makes for a dull and static composition. You may also find that you need to break up the horizontals in some way, perhaps by including a figure standing on the beach or the mast of a boat providing a link between sea and sky.

The most common mistake of all is failure to suggest the sea as a horizontal plane (this applies to all paintings of water). Although you will sometimes observe a great variety of colors and tones you will have to control them carefully so that you suggest recession (see landscape: perspective). Keep the blues and grays cooler toward the horizon and reserve the stronger contrasts of tone for the shoreline.

WAVES STEP-BY-STEP

1 Working quickly in the *alla prima* style, the artist covers the entire canvas with a toned ground of titanium white mixed with a trace of Prussian blue. Using a ¹/₂ in. (1.27 cm) decorator's brush, he applies the paint thinly and in curving, arc-like sweeps, which will later help to accentuate the sense of dynamic movement in the foam burst. The sea is quickly painted with mixtures of Prussian blue, Hooker's green, and cadmium yellow, applied with vigorous, broken strokes that suggest the choppy movement of the waves.

This is where most of the "action" is, with waves breaking, and advancing water pushing foam over shiny wet sand. The colors to be seen in water close to you are exciting and often quite unexpected – ochers and browns caused by sand mixing with water; violets and blues caused by reflections from the sky. These effects can often be suggested by working wet into wet, so that the colors blend softly together, and using large brush strokes that follow the direction of the water's movement.

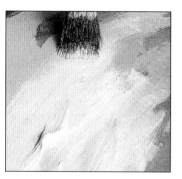

2 The shape and form of the foam burst are now developed. Titanium white is mixed with a little medium to a thick, creamy consistency and applied with heavy impasto strokes, particularly at the base of the wave. Using the ½ in. (1.27 cm) decorator's brush, the artist scumbles the color quickly so that it blends partially with the cool undertone. This gives a sense of volume to the foam burst by indicating areas of light and shade.

3 Now the artist uses the edge of a painting knife to lay in long, broken strokes of titanium white at the upper edge of the foam burst. These strokes of solid, creamy color create a dramatic outline against the sky and heighten the impression of the great forces with which the foam splashes upward.

4 The decorator's brush is used to spatter titanium white across the shape of the foam burst to imply broken flecks of foam and further emphasize the directional movement of the wave.

5 The completed picture gives a thrilling impression of the explosive forces of nature. Heavy impasto and bold, vigorous brush strokes are used in the point of impact – the lower area of the foam, where there is more weight and density. The outer edges of the foam are dispersed by the wind and become more translucent, blending into the surrounding atmosphere. This contrast of sharp and blurred passages gives movement and atmosphere to the painting.

BOATS

Unlike cars, which many people ruthlessly edit out of urban scenes because they "spoil the view," boats are delightful to look at, and seem very much a part of seascapes, lakes, and river scenes. However, their swelling curves are not easy to draw, particularly when they are foreshortened or tipped on one side as when on a beach.

During the initial drawing stage you will find it helpful to think of the boat as a shape that can fit into a rectangular box. Begin by drawing the mid-line from bow to stern, as in this way you can ensure that the two sides are precisely equal. Now lightly draw the imaginary box, and fit the rest of the boat into it.

If you are fairly close the rules of perspective will help you with parallel planking, seating, cabin tops, and so on. The height of masts and other uprights can be checked by comparison with the overall length of the boat. Hold up a pencil or paintbrush at arm's length and slide your thumb up and down it to assess heights, and hold it horizontally to measure widths.

A boat in the water is also frequently seen at an angle, as it will often be pitching or riding a wave. If the water is still you will not have this problem, but it is important to observe exactly how much of the hull is showing and how much higher it is at one point than another. Reflections are vital here, as they not only make the water look more convincing but indicate the exact position at which the boat enters the water.

LAMADINE by David Curtis

The shapes made by the waves as they gather, peak, and break into spray have been carefully observed and painted with a sure and confident hand and brush strokes that describe the movement. Both the sails and the white, sunlit patches of cloud echo the breakers, continuing the movement into the sky to create an overall effect of drama.

BUILDINGS AND ARCHITECTURE

Inexperienced painters often avoid architectural subjects because they feel unable to cope with the complexities of perspective, but this is a pity as buildings play such a large part in the 21st-century landscape. It is certainly helpful to have some understanding of the basic rules of perspective, but they are not really very difficult to grasp.

Perspective is no more than a convention that allows you to represent a solid, three-dimensional object on a two-dimensional surface, and the only really important rule is that all objects appear to become smaller the farther away they are. This creates the illusion that parallel lines receding from you meet each other at a "vanishing point" at your eye level. If you are looking down on a scene from a hilltop the lines will slope upward to your eye level, but if you are positioned below a building on rising ground they will slope downward, sometimes quite sharply.

Often this vanishing point is outside the picture area, but bearing the rule in mind helps you to check your own on-the-spot observations. If you rely on your eye alone you may find yourself painting what you think you see instead of what is actually there – it is often difficult to believe the sharpness of the angle made by receding parallels. When making an underdrawing for a painting it is sound practice to mark in the horizon line (your eye level), as here the receding lines will be horizontal, and they will provide a key for all the others.

MECHANICAL AIDS

When you are painting a single building perspective is easy enough, but for a complex cityscape it can present problems, and always has. Canaletto (1697–1768) is known to have used a device called a camera obscura, which projected the image onto paper through a system of lenses so that an accurate outline drawing could be made with the minimum of effort. Many of the topographical artists of the 18th and early 19th centuries carried similar unwieldy objects around with them, but today we are more fortunate as we have the benefit of the camera. Photographs are not always the ideal starting point for paintings, as they tend to fudge detail and often fail to catch the subtleties of color, but they certainly have their uses. You might, for example, make an underdrawing from a photograph and then go out to complete the painting on location. Or you can use photographs in combination with on-the-spot sketches and color notes as a basis for a studio painting.

OUTDOORS OR IN

Working directly from your subject is very appealing, but it does present certain problems, particularly for urban subjects. It can be difficult to find a place to paint where you have an interesting view of the subject and are relatively safe from the comments of passersby. It is wise to explore various locations before setting out with your easel and paints. You can often find a quiet corner, or you could ask permission to sit on the roof of a

building to paint an aerial view; Oscar Kokoschka (1886–1980) did this in several European cities.

The other major problem is coping with changing light. On a fine day the colors of both the sunstruck and shaded areas will change dramatically as the sun moves higher (or lower) in the sky, and shadows will also change shape quite rapidly. Never try to finish a whole painting in one day, as you will find yourself making alterations to keep up with the changing light, and this is a recipe for failure. Either set aside about two hours at the same time each day and work in a series of sessions, or make quick sketches which you can then work up into a

LEFT OF WHITE HALL LOOKING NORTH by Antonio Canaletto (c. 1730)

Antonio Canaletto is probably best known for his views of the canals and buildings of Venice. He often painted at great speed for the tourist market. He as certainly skillful and, at his best, a thoughtful and objective observer in a realistic tradition.

composition indoors.

Many painters of architectural subjects take the latter course, and their pictures are none the worse for it. However, the way you choose to work depends very much on individual interests, and if your main concern is light and atmosphere rather than structure and precise detail there is no substitute for working *alla prima* directly from your subject.

VIEWPOINT

Your choice of viewpoint should depend on three main factors. First,

you must consider exactly what aspect of your chosen subject you wish to portray, and perhaps emphasize. Is it a specific building or the relationship of buildings in a street that interests you? Perhaps it may be the overall color or character of the street itself you want to capture, or the way the buildings throw a strong pattern of shadows across the ground and walls.

The second consideration is composition. Even slight changes in your own position can cause dramatic ones in the view in front of you, so be careful to explore all available possibilities. A good composition is a

CA D'ORO, VENICE by Richard Beer

Painting buildings from directly in front has a tendency to make them look flat, but in this case the viewpoint has been well-chosen, as the artist wanted to emphasize their decorative quality. Depth is given to the picture almost solely by the perspective created by the blue posts. The expanse of water, occupying over half the picture area, provides a counterfoil for the lovely intricate arches and balconies.

THE SEVERN VALLEY FROM MALVERN by Stephen Crowther

The elevated viewpoint taken here enabled the artist to make the most of the foreground garden and the roofs, which would otherwise have been hidden. A great expanse of landscape in the background was also visible, sweeping away to the distant strip of sky.

well-balanced one, and if you have chosen a viewpoint that shows you a large, dark house on the left with nothing to balance it your painting will look wrong. This does not have to be another house; it could be a suitably shaped shadow, a tree, clouds, or even a small shape such as a figure as long as it makes up for lack of size by being a strong value or color.

The third consideration is purely practical. For example, you cannot station yourself in the middle of a road (where, unfortunately, the best viewpoints are often found). The view from a window is sometimes ideal, and has the added advantage of peace and seclusion.

COMPOSITION

Because architectural subjects are among the more difficult, there is a tendency to forget about the purely pictorial values in the effort to get the proportion and perspective right and all the doors and windows in the correct place. But composition is important whatever you are painting, so if you are working on location take a critical look at what is in front of you and try to decide how you can place the various elements to the best advantage.

There are no absolute rules about composition, but in general you should aim for a good

balance of shapes, colors, and dark and light areas, and enough variety to encourage the viewer's eye to look from one part of the picture to another.

It is not usually a good idea to divide a picture in half or to place the main subject – such as a house – right in the middle of the picture area. Symmetrical arrangements are usually static and dull.

THE TEA STALL, SOUTHWOLD by Raymond Leech

The high angle chosen here (see viewpoint) has allowed the artist to make an unusual and dynamic composition with a pleasing balance of diagonals and verticals. When planning a painting it is always worth exploring different possibilities – the most obvious view is not always the best.

VILLAGE CHURCH, PROVENCE by
David Donaldson

To some extent your composition will have already been determined by the place you have chosen to paint from (see viewpoint). However, it is highly likely that you will have to do some fine-tuning, and you will also need to decide how much of the subject to include.

A viewfinder is a great help here. Some artists like to take an empty picture frame out with them so that they can hold it up and explore various possibilities, but you can make your own viewfinder simply by cutting a rectangular window in a piece of cardboard.

The obvious center of interest here is the church, with its striking geometric tower, but the artist has taken care to place it off-center and to balance it with the contrasting round mass of the tree on the left. The extreme foreground has been painted loosely in order to steal interest from the church, but the bold, linear treatment of the plants and grasses leads our eye toward it, as does the directional brushwork on the tree.

GIRL IN A RED DRESS by Raymond Leech

The vital ingredient of this unusual composition is the steps, whose form and repetitive shape lead the eye into the picture to the central lamppost and eye-catching red dress. They have been very carefully painted, as has the area of wall behind with its pattern of large slabs. This also plays an important part in the picture.

DETAIL

Once you begin to focus in on a building to see what it is that gives it its special character you will see a wealth of detail, such as balconies, cornices, window frames and sills, patterns of brickwork, and drainpipes twisting down a wall, and you will have to decide how much to include.

There is no reason why you should not put in everything you see, but equally there is no reason why you should.

Remember that the painting is the important thing, and if the composition needs an accent of color in the form of a brightly painted door or a curtained window then make the most of such things.

You might also consider taking a close-up approach and homing in on one small part of a building, such as an open door or a single window. Such subjects can make very exciting compositions, but you will have to plan the composition with care to avoid an overly symmetrical effect – symmetry is static and thus does not hold the viewer's interest.

Think about placing a window off-center or painting it at an angle so that you have diagonal as well as vertical and horizontal lines. You might also stress texture and pattern, such as that of the brick- or stonework surrounding a window or door.

GARDEN TOPIARY by Glenn Scouller

Very few precise architectural details have been included here. The artist's interest lay in the overall pattern created by the repeated shapes of the shutters with their slanting shadows and the two parallel gateposts with their triangular red tops. The latter have been echoed by the stylized conical bushes to the right, which are obviously contrived for the sake of the painting, as are the palm trees whose semi-circular fronds provide curves to balance the more angular shapes. The paint surface is equally exciting. Rich texture has been built up on the white wall by a combination of brush impasto and knife painting, while the sgraffito method has been used on the right-hand bush to make linear marks which reveal an earlier layer of vivid color.

THE ANIMAL WORLD

Animals have a reputation for being difficult to paint, mainly because they tend to move most of the time. But capturing the grace and agility of an animal – especially a moving animal – is one of the most rewarding experiences an artist can have. Painting animals does not require a textbook knowledge of their anatomy; intelligent observation, sensitivity, and a basic awareness of form and structure will suffice, plus a willingness to practice! By all means study pictures in books and magazines, but it is generally not a good idea to make a painting by copying from a photograph, because photographs tend to flatten form and reduce detail; invariably the resulting painting lacks life and movement. If you have a pet, then you have endless opportunities for sketching and painting it. If not, try to visit a zoo or wildlife park, where you can observe the characteristic movements and gestures of a wide variety of animals.

Even though they are moving, you will find that most animals tend to repeat certain gestures; a good tactic is to work on several sketches at once, shifting from one to the other as the animal alters and regains certain positions. This may be frustrating at first, but gradually your reflexes will quicken and you will soon learn how to capture the essential character of

the animal you are portraying. In addition, making studies of the stuffed animals in museums of natural history will give you an opportunity to examine, at close quarters, their fascinating textures and markings.

The most common mistake seen in animal paintings is that the creature appears to be "stuck on" to the picture surface, or floating in mid-air. One way to overcome this problem is to establish the value and color of the background first, working around the approximate outline of the animal. It is always easier to integrate the subject into the background than vice versa. Another way to avoid the "cut-out" look is by using a variety of hard and soft edges; where the form of the animal is in shadow, the outline will be "lost" or blurred, and where it meets the light it will be sharp. This combination of hard and soft edges makes the animal appear to blend naturally with its surroundings.

Another point to bear in mind is that too much attention to detail can freeze a rendering of an animal and make it appear stuffed. To convey a sense of life and movement, it is often a good idea to give a high degree of finish to the main features and a sketchy quality to the others. This will give added force to your painting, and also leave something to the viewer's imagination.

HOW TO PAINT FUR

Fur – just like human hair – comes in a wide variety of textures. How you render these depends on the type of animal you are portraying, the medium you are working with, and whether the animal is to be seen close-up or in the distance. Below are some examples of suitable techniques, but it is wise to remember that you should always start by defining the outline of the animal, then suggest the pattern of light and shade on its body, and lastly, pay attention to the markings and individual features.

For animals with a sleek, glossy coat, use a wet-in-wet technique. Observe the patterns of light and shadow carefully, then paint them with fast, fluid brush strokes. Use as few strokes as possible, to accentuate the glossiness of the coat.

For animals with a fluffy, shaggy or wiry coat, use scumbling or drybrush with a bristle brush and fairly thick, dry paint. Another method, often used in watercolor and gouache, is to block in the colors and tones of the coat with broad washes; when this is dry, use the tip of the finely pointed brush to tick in tiny lines that follow the pattern of hair growth. This technique is effective for rendering short-haired animals such as dogs and foxes.

Some animals, such as horses, cows, deer, and smooth-haired dog breeds, have a short, sleek, and velvety coat. The muscular structure beneath the coat is much more pronounced than in long-haired animals, so attention must be paid to the subtle modeling of values. You could start by defining the form with a series of watery washes, and then suggest the lie of the coat with very short strokes using a finely pointed brush.

PAINTING FUR STEP-BY-STEP

1 Layers of pigment have been applied thinly to build up the depth of color and the details of the hairs are added on top, using a fine brush to smudge in the color.

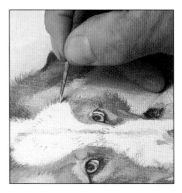

2 White hairs are added with a No. 0 sable brush, painting each individual hair slowly and methodically

The finished effect.

3 The pencil marks of the underdrawing indicate the folds of the dog's flesh and the way the fur stands out. In the final picture, below, the pencil marks are strengthened and flake white is added to pick out the fur against the background.

PAINTING FEATHERS

Use a prepared primed surface for your oil painting. Start by blocking in the main areas of color with thin paint that has been well diluted with turpentine. Introduce thicker color, adding the wings and feathers and gradually building up the strength of the values of the body and heads of the birds. Oil paint is more flexible than acrylic and takes much longer to dry. This means that the paint can be blended and manipulated on the picture surface for several hours after it has been applied. Take advantage of this property to build up the picture surface in a lively way, and to create an interesting, textural finish to the paint. Use a painting knife to apply broad, flat areas of solid color, using the side and point of the knife to scratch in the fine, wispy effect of the feathers. The finished oil painting is richly colored and densely textured, with the linear detail applied in solid strong colors to consolidate the fur and give a feeling of solidity and substance to the subject.

PAINTING A WILD ANIMAL STEP-BY-STEP

To translate the animal's movement into the painting, pick out characteristic curves and angles in the body and legs. Watch the animal carefully as it moves, looking for repeated movements. Utilize the texture of your brush strokes to describe thick fur, feathers or other textures and lay in small touches of color in the earth tones to enliven the overall image. Keep the background simple to focus attention on the color and patterns within the animal.

It can be interesting to use more than one animal in a painting, as the artist can then show more than one position, movement or type of behavior. Photographs, other pictures, or rough sketches made "on location" can be used as a base, with the various animals or positions of the same animal being combined into the final picture.

1 Draw up the outline shape in charcoal. Block in basic areas of tone with yellow ocher and blue-black.

2 Sketch in the pattern of stripes in blue-black, using a small bristle brush. Scrub in thin layers of color over the whole picture.

3 Work quickly over the shape of the animal with yellow, burnt sienna, and white laying color into the black pattern. Angle the brush marks to accentuate form.

4 Adjust the proportions of the drawing and the division of the picture plane. Strengthen the blacks and heighten the colors, adding touches of red and blue.

5 Develop the tonal range in the background, spreading the paint with a rag. Work with black and brown to make a dense area of shadow.

6 Continue to work up the colors, dabbing in the shapes with a bristle brush, well loaded with paint to make a rich texture.

PORTRAITS AND FIGURES

Painting people – whether portraits, full-length figures, or groups – is one of the most challenging and satisfying of all branches of art. It is also the one most often associated with oil painting. This is partly because most of the portraits and figure studies of the past have been in oils, but there is a more practical reason too. Drawing and painting people is not easy, and using oils, which can be scraped down, overpainted, and corrected in a number of ways, allows you to make false starts without being bound by them.

CHANGING STYLES

The ways in which figures have been portrayed over the centuries has varied enormously, partly because of a shifting emphasis in patronage. The pre-Renaissance artists, dependant on the Church for their commissions, were limited to exclusively religious subject matter, and their depictions of the Holy Family and various saints were idealized versions of humanity – the physical imperfections of actual human beings would not have been acceptable. These, however, began to appear in the works of such artists as Masaccio (1401–1428),

Leonardo da Vinci (1452–1519), and Raphael (1483–1520).

During the time of the last three, it was believed that figure painting had reached its peak and could not be bettered. In a way it certainly had, and Renaissance art still has much to teach us today, but in terms of style we have moved on. The figures in Michelangelo's Sistine ceiling have tremendous power and drama, but these are no longer major concerns. Most people would now find a portrait by Whistler (1834–1902)

THE DELPHIC SYBIL by
Michelangelo

*Michelangelo worked on the
Sistine ceiling between 1508 and
1512. The Sybil's head and eyes
turn away from the movement of
her arms, her strong body, and
face derived from classical
sculpture.*

more immediately appealing
and lifelike, though his
pictures were scorned by
contemporaries as sketchy
and unfinished looking.

One of the most famous
of all nude studies, Olympia
by Edouard Manet
(1832–1883), caused an
outcry when it was
exhibited at the Salon. The nude had
previously been acceptable only when
placed in a historical or mythological
setting, but Manet's model was an
ordinary Parisian girl, and the picture
exudes sexuality.

In those not very far-off days there
were rules, not only about subject
matter, but also about how to paint –
Manet was much criticized for his
technique, in particular his lack of
tonal modeling. We are fortunate in
having no such standards imposed
upon us. Looking around any major
art gallery demonstrates the way each
new generation has brought its own
theories and interests to bear on the
subject of the human figure, and it is
now obvious that there is no "best"

way to paint figures or portraits – it
depends on what the individual artist
wants to say.

THE IMPORTANCE OF DRAWING

But however free and spontaneous
portrait or figure study may look, it
has to be based on sound knowledge
and observation, so get into the habit
of drawing and sketching people
whenever you can, and when you
start on a painting, try to see the
figure as a set of simple forms that
join together, not as a collection of
small details. In a portrait, look for the
main planes of the head created by
the forehead and temples, the bridge

213

SYDNEY FROM STEPNEY by Olwen Tarrant

This simple, classic composition ensures that attention if focused on the sitter's character, and the somber mood is enhanced by the very limited color range. When planning a head and shoulders composition care must be taken to leave sufficient space at the top and sides of the head or it may look cramped and uncomfortable

and sides of the nose, eye sockets, cheekbones, and chin. One way to observe these while excluding details is blur your vision by half closing your eyes. This will also enable you to assess the main shape of a face and its overall color, the two most important basics.

Be careful about proportions, as these are the downfall of many inexperienced painters. Legs and arms, for example, are longer than you would think, and feet and hands larger. Proportions can be measured by

holding up a pencil or ruler and sliding your thumb up and down it, a time-honored method used by most artists — some even use a pair of dividers for very precise measurements.

Once you have worked out the composition, make a careful underdrawing on the support before you start to apply color. You may find it helpful to do an underpainting as well, as this will help you to establish the main masses of color and tone. The golden rule is not to rush; the more care you take in the early stages the freer you can be in the later ones.

COMPOSING A PORTRAIT

A portrait is first and foremost a painting, and should be treated with as much regard for composition, color and so on as any other subject. To fulfill its function as a portrait it must also portray a specific personality, so you will need to consider how the composition can bring this out.

Decisions must be made about the position of the head, the clothing, how much of the person's body to show (you could stop at the shoulders or continue down to the hands), the background, and any other objects you may want to include.

Study your sitter to ascertain what are his or her most distinctive qualities.

THE NEW BABY
by Stephen
Crowther

*The window bars
provide a
background frame
for the delicate
treatment of the
sitter's head, and
the green foliage in
the garden beyond
stresses the theme of
new life. The pose, with the tilting head and the hand resting on the baby's body, expresses
quiet devotion, but the composition is full of movement.*

It is usually easier to begin with someone you know well, as you will have made some of these observations already. Most people have characteristic ways of holding their heads and hands, and tend to sit in particular positions. They cannot assume these to order, but will gradually fall into them if allowed to relax and become used to being stared at.

Choose a color scheme for the picture, but remember that it is usually best to keep the clothing and background fairly muted so that they do not compete with the face, which is always the focal point in a portrait. Experiment with the lighting, making sure that the shadows are cast in a way that defines the form of the features and any important creases or dimples. In general it is best to avoid very harsh lighting as this can make the sitter look gaunt and old, and robs the shadows of color.

215

PROFESSOR MICHAEL SHEPHERD by Rupert Shephard

This formal portrait has been built up gradually in layers over an underpainting. The face has been described in considerable detail, but there are very few hard edges, the only relatively sharp contours being those of the nostril and the lips.

ACHIEVING A LIKENESS

The general shapes of faces vary much more widely than most people realize. You do not have to go right up to people to identify them; even at a distance a face can be distinguished as that of a specific person. You can also usually recognize a blurred photograph without any trouble.

It thus follows that the first thing to do in a portrait is to establish the shape of the face and the underlying structure: the planes of the forehead and temples and of the bridge and sides of the nose; the position of the eye sockets, cheek-bones, and chin.

The next step is to take careful measure-ments to establish these planes and their relationship to one another on canvas. Details, such as eyebrows and the precise line of lips, should always be built up to slowly; if you begin with these you are less likely to produce a good portrait. You may even find that you can stop working on the picture far sooner than you had originally envisaged and

FARRELL CLEARY by Susan Wilson

This powerful portrait, with its loose, bold brushwork, makes an interesting contrast with Rupert Shephard's opposite. The posture and face are beautifully observed, and the composition is given additional strength by the firm black lines against the flat neutral background.

with fewer details than you would have thought necessary. If this is the case, resist the temptation to continue, as you could ruin the painting.

217

PAINTING CHILDREN

TIMMY by Jeremy Galton

Painted in exactly two hours, the intention of this alla prima portrait was to capture a pose and expression characteristic of this child, the artist's son. Some very thin underpainting established the main framework of the face, and this was followed by just one layer of thicker paint. The painting was done on hardboard stained an ocher color, and this colored ground, visible over much of the face, contributes to the finished effect.

PORTRAIT OF EMMA by David Curtis

The proportions of the face and body of a child are quite different from those of an adult, and the contours of the face are smoother. These big blue eyes set in a smooth pink face, and the narrow shoulders and short arms, could only belong to a child. The soft hat and muted colors enhance the impression of youthful innocence.

218

Painting children, particularly those related to you, is extremely rewarding, as each picture becomes a personal record of the child's growth.

A difficulty is, of course, the child's notorious inability to keep still. Some artists solve this problem by bribery, while others try to catch their "sitter" when he or she is fully absorbed in some activity, such as drawing, reading, playing with trains or dolls, or even watching television. The latter course has a dual advantage; first the child will appear relaxed and will unconsciously adopt some typical pose or gesture, and second the activity will tell a story about the child's particular interests at the time.

Children tend to look stiff and embarrassed if asked to pose for any length of time, which does not make for a good portrait. Thus if you do intend completing a whole painting in front of the sitter you will have to be prepared to work quickly in short sessions. If you normally make an underpainting, it is helpful in such cases to use acrylic for this, as it dries in a matter of minutes.

One of the most common mistakes is making the child look too old, which can happen if you even slightly overwork any dimples or shadows. It is best to keep the lighting soft, and avoid too much contrast of light and dark. The contours of the face are much gentler in children than in adults, so you may want to avoid obvious brush strokes – the finger painting method could be useful, at least in some areas of the picture.

BOY AND GIRL ON BEACH by
Arthur Maderson

The placing of the children high in the picture enhances their slightness of build and also excludes the spectator from their private, whispering world by placing the water between them and us.

GLOSSARY

Abstract Relying on color, pattern and form rather than the realistic or naturalistic portrayal of subject matter.

Aerial Perspective The use of color and tone to indicate space and recession.

Alla Prima Direct painting in which the picture is completed in one session without any underpainting or underdrawing.

Binder A liquid medium that is mixed with powdered pigment to form a paint.

Blending Merging adjacent color areas so that the transition between the colors is imperceptible.

Blocking In The first stage of a painting, in which the main forms of the composition are laid down in approximate areas of tone and color.

Broken Color A term used in color theory to describe a color mixed from two secondary colors.

Chroma The degree of brightness or dullness of a color.

Composition The organization of color and form within a picture area.

Complementary Colors The colors that appear at opposite sides of the color wheel.

Diluent A liquid such as turpentine that is used to dilute paint. It evaporates completely and has no binding effect on the pigment.

Dry Brush In this technique dry paint is dragged across the surface of a painting, so that it adheres to the raised areas, creating broken areas of color.

Glazing The application of a transparent film of color over a lighter, opaque color. It is sometimes used to modify darker colors.

Ground A ground or priming is a surface which has been specially prepared to accept oil paint.

Hue This term indicates the type of color in terms of its blueness, redness, or yellowness. About 150 different hues can be recognized.

Impasto Paint applied thickly so that it retains the mark of the brush or the knife.

Lean A term used to describe oil paint which has little or no added oil. The expression "fat over lean" refers to the use of lean paint (thinned with turpentine or mineral spirits) under paint layers into which more oil is progressively introduced. This method of working prevents the paint surface from cracking as it dries.

Linear Perspective A method of creating an illusion of depth and three dimensions on a flat surface through the use of converging lines and vanishing points.

Mahl Stick A cane used for steadying the painting arm when putting in fine detail. One end is covered with a soft pad to prevent the point from damaging the support.

Mask Tape or paper used to isolate a particular area of a painting. This allows the artist to work freely in the rest of the painting.

Medium The material used for painting or drawing, such as watercolor, pencil, or oil paint.

Opacity The ability of a pigment to cover and obscure the surface or color to which it is applied.

Optical Color Mixing Creating new colors by mixing pigments optically on the canvas rather than on the palette.

Painting Knife A knife with a thin flexible blade used for applying paint to a support. These knives generally have a cranked handle and are available in a range of shapes and sizes.

Palette Knife A knife with a straight steel blade used for mixing paint on the palette, cleaning the palette and, if necessary, scraping paint from the support.

Picture Plane The imaginary vertical plane that separates the viewer's world from that of the picture.

Planes The flat surfaces of an object. These are revealed by light and dark. Even a curved surface can be regarded as an infinite number of small places.

Primary Color These are colors that cannot be obtained by mixing other colors. The paint primaries are red, yellow, and blue.

Priming Also known as ground, this is the layer or layers of materials applied to a support to make it less absorbent or more pleasant to paint on.

Renaissance The cultural revival of classical ideals that took place in Europe from the fourteenth to the sixteenth centuries.

Sgraffito This is a technique in which the artist scratches through a layer of paint to reveal another paint layer beneath – or to reveal the support.

Scumbling Dryish, opaque paint that is brushed freely over preceding layers so that the underlying color, or the support, shows through in places.

Size Gelatinous solution, such as rabbit-skin glue, which is used to seal the support.

Stipple The use of dots in painting, drawing, or engraving, instead of line or flat color.

Support A surface for painting or drawing, which could be canvas, board or paper.

Underdrawing The preliminary drawing for a painting, often done in pencil, charcoal, or paint.

Underpainting The preliminary blocking-in of the main forms, colors, and tonal areas.

Value The degree of lightness or darkness. The value of a color is assessed independently of its hue.

Wash An application of thinly diluted paint.

Wet into Dry The application of paint to a completely dry surface.

Wet in Wet The application of wet paint to an already wet surface. Used in the *alla prima* technique. Wet in wet allows the artist to blend colors and tones.

INDEX

PICTURE CREDITS

The material in this book previously appeared in:

Oil Painters Question and Answer Book; Color How to see it, How to paint it; Painting Shapes and Edges; The Complete Drawing & Painting Course; Complete Watercolor Artist; The Complete Artist; The Encyclopedia of Oil Painting Techniques; Painting Techniques; Painting with Oils; The Complete Watercolor Artist; The Oil Painter's Pocket Palette; The Artist's Manual; How to Paint Trees, Flowers & Foliage; Light – How to see it – How to paint it; Tonal Values – How to see them, how to paint them; How to Draw & Paint; The Encyclopedia of Flower Painting Techniques; You Can Paint Portraits; You Can Paint Flowers, Plants & Nature.